IGNORANCE ON FIRE

Heath Oakes

Clovercroft Publishing

Ignorance on Fire

© 2017 by Heath Oakes

Published by Clovercroft Publishing, Franklin, Tennessee

Published in association with Larry Carpenter of Christian Book Services, LLC www.christianbookservices.com

Edited by Robert Irvin

Cover Design by Debbie Manning Sheppard

Interior Design by Suzanne Lawing

Printed in the United States of America

978-1-942557-87-6

DEDICATION

This book is:
To those who have had the vision to lead and mentor me.
To those who have had the courage to follow me.
For those seeking the vision and courage to lead themselves and
others to do great things.

ACKNOWLEDGMENT

My great thanks to Roy Jeffords for believing in my vision and
helping me turn this book into reality.

CONTENTS

Resources

INTRODUCTION

During senior year, my high school classmates picked the person Most Likely to Succeed; I finished in last place. I had a lot of fun growing up, but I was never one to toe the line, and nobody ever accused me of being a good student. In spite of all that, I was just twenty-three when I became the youngest territory sales manager ever promoted by the seventy-two-year-old Fortune 500 company I worked for.

When my new boss told me I had the job, I packed everything I owned into my best friend's black Chevy Silverado and headed to Jacksonville, Florida. Driving down Interstate-10, I couldn't help but smile, thinking how surprised everybody must be. None, however, more than me.

I always said I'd never leave East Texas. On top of that, just eighteen months earlier, flush with success as an independent agent and manager, I had sworn on a stack of Bibles that I would never be somebody's employee again. Especially in corporate America. A mid-six-figure income made a strong argument for me to take this promotion, however. Also, the new position gave me the chance to help a lot of people achieve their dreams.

I was taking over the North Florida Territory, the second-lowest performing organization in the country. That meant very few people were making a living with our company in that area. It also meant I had plenty of hard work ahead of me. On the plus side, this sales territory and I had something in common. Nobody expected either of us to succeed.

I like to win, mostly because I really hate to lose, and moving to Jacksonville seemed like a losing proposition to a lot of people. I wasn't worried. Helping a team succeed has become a habit for me, but it didn't happen until after I'd learned some important lessons about life.

A big one was that my success would come from helping other people achieve their own dreams. That one idea changed not just *my* life, but the lives of folks I've been fortunate enough to work with. The second thing I learned is that the first lesson is a hard one. It takes leadership, and leadership means *giving*. I wasn't sure I could ever wrap my head around that one, but three specific lessons I learned about life and leadership along the way helped me go beyond many of the expectations I had starting out.

We Millennials sometimes have a bad reputation with the generations that came before us, but so did every other generation as it entered adulthood. Whatever our age, we make our world a better place when we help each other. That's why I'm sharing these lessons—experiences that have helped me and so many others.

ONE

A PURPLE VELVET SUIT

I jammed my finger against the cell phone screen and waited for my mom to answer. I was angry, humiliated, and, at nineteen years old, felt truly defeated for the first time in my life. More than anything, I needed the wisdom of my parents, and it seemed like each ring stretched out for hours while I waited, willing Mom to answer.

My parents have always been my strongest supporters. Even when I decided to leave college and step into the world on my own, they were close by, cheering me along. When we were growing up, that kind of support was about all they could give my brother and me. We lived in a single-wide trailer parked on a rented piece of land so far out of town we had to pipe in sunlight.

My brother and I never went without what we needed, but we had to earn everything extra ourselves. Growing up,

I always wanted more—more fun, more wins on the ball field, more money—and I would overcome any obstacle to get what I was after. More than once, my parents watched me fail my way forward until I achieved my goal.

That terrible afternoon when I was nineteen was the first time either of them had seen me ready to give up.

Graduationg from high school, my plan was to pursue a career in law enforcement. That meant I had to earn a certain number of college credits. But I'd gone to school for two reasons—sports and girls. Classes were just something I had to do so I could hang out with my friends. Even if a school would accept me, a classroom was the last place I wanted to be.

I wound up at the community college in Tyler, Texas. After three semesters, I had enough hours to enter the criminal justice academy. There was just one problem. The minimum age to become a police officer was twenty-one, and I was nineteen. I had to figure out a way to support myself until I became legal.

Finding a paycheck wasn't a problem. Oil is big business in East Texas, and back then jobs were waiting for guys who could do the work. The money was good, but an oil field job meant long stretches away from home. Even if it was only until I turned twenty-one, that wasn't the life I wanted. Something else was out there.

I heard an ad on the radio one day about a local car dealership hiring five new salespeople. They were paying a five-hundred-dollar signing bonus. That got my attention! Also, my dad's brother worked at the same dealership ten years earlier. He died about nine months before I saw that ad, and his loss still hurt.

My uncle and I had become close when he moved back to East Texas a few years earlier. While he was away, he would show up at our house about once a year, always in a new Corvette, his newest girlfriend riding shotgun. He was larger than life, and he always dressed the part. I remember one of his suits was purple velvet, and he spent more money on shoes than some families earned in a month.

Those yearly visits gave me just a glimpse of the world that existed beyond Troup, Texas, where I grew up. From the little I'd seen, I figured that outside world had everything I wanted in life. Success would mean achieving the same glitzy, fast-paced lifestyle my uncle enjoyed.

Working at a dealership he used to manage seemed like a pretty good starting place, so just a couple of weeks after I left college I bought a ten-dollar pair of dress shoes from a bargain bin store and headed down there for an interview. Since my uncle didn't always leave a job under the best circumstances, I decided not to mention our connection. It might have really helped me, but it just as easily could have hurt my chances.

Not only did I get the job, I sold a car the day I started. Within a few weeks, I was the dealership's top salesman. My commission check that first month was more money than I'd ever made in a year.

It was so big I forgot all about that career in law enforcement.

The next month proved even better, and the money kept rolling in. Without realizing it, I became that kid who did good. I was already earning more money than my parents ever had, and my friends and family looked up to me as a success story. I followed my uncle's example and invested in clothes and shoes to look the part. I didn't have a purple velvet suit, but I learned how to dress with some swag. Life was good.

Still, everything wasn't sunshine and roses. I didn't know

what, exactly, but something was off. As exciting as the income was, watching how business was done on the car lot made me question my uncle's example. In the furthest reaches of my mind, I began to wonder if success might involve something more than a big income.

Having a life away from work seemed like it would be one of the best things about finding success. It was one of the reasons I took the job at the dealership instead of going out to the oil fields. It didn't take long to learn that being a car salesman isn't all that different from being a roughneck when it comes to having a life. Also, in my quest to become wealthy, I talked to everyone I could about the best way to achieve my goals. One thing I constantly heard was that building real wealth requires at least one stream of residual income.

If you've ever done retail sales or something like real estate, you know what happens the second you quit selling: your income stops. That's a pretty simple thing to understand, even for a lazy nineteen-year-old kid who wanted to make a fast buck and retire early. I needed to earn what's known in the sales industry as mailbox money—that's a paycheck that shows up every month, whether you're actually working or not. So I started hunting for an opportunity that would let me make the income I wanted and still enjoy a life away from work.

As I was starting my search, one of my dad's friends told me about the insurance industry. He explained how an agent's paycheck is based on his willingness to work, and how today's effort turns into tomorrow's renewal income. That's mailbox money!

He probably told me how much a good insurance agent can help people too, but all I heard was the dollars. It sounded exactly like what I was looking for, so I checked out some job listings and landed an interview with a local agency.

My nerves were tight when I walked into that meeting. Being from East Texas, my accent is so thick that sometimes even I can't understand what I'm saying. Despite being pretty successful to that point, I knew I was still a young country boy who hadn't learned his city manners yet.

As it turned out, however, I had nothing to worry about. I had the job before I left. They thought I was all that and a slice of bread! My boots didn't touch the ground on the way back to my truck.

It was disappointing to learn later that they hired *everybody* who was willing to go door to door selling insurance policies on straight commission. Right then, though, the future was mine to take.

TWO

OOPS, I DIDN'T THINK OF THAT

Have you ever been truly excited about something, like passing a test or getting a new job, then come crashing back down to earth when you thought about exactly what came next? That's how it felt when I realized I had to tell my sales manager, Jeff, that I was leaving the car business.

The best time to have the conversation would have been when I got to work on Thursday morning. Instead, I decided he looked too busy and chickened out. I blew my next opportunity as well, on Friday, since we had some traffic, and I didn't want to miss any sales.

I finally went to his office on Saturday morning, the absolute busiest time for any car dealership.

On my way down the hall, I passed the sales board where we tracked each salesperson's deals. The person at the top of the board was the leader, while the one at the bottom brought up the rear. The name at the top? Heath Oakes.

Jeff was at his desk, buried in paperwork, when I rapped on the door and stepped into his office.

"I don't think this is for me," I said, trying to keep my voice from cracking.

He mumbled something, but didn't look up from his work.

"This isn't what I want to do," I said, trying a second time to get his attention. "I found something else."

That got Jeff to look up. He stared at me and then pointed to the board in the hall. With a blank look on his face, he said, "What do you mean this is not for you? You're at the top of the board. You're always at the top of the board." He blinked. "What are you talking about?"

I shrugged and looked down at my shoes, the nicest, most expensive pair I'd ever owned. "I don't know, man. It's just not for me."

Jeff got up and closed the door, then waved me into a chair. He waited until I sat, then said, "You're a natural at this. What's going on?"

"I just want something more," I told him. "I mean, I'm here all the time, and when I'm not, I'm worried about the sales I'm missing."

"So, what is it you want to do?"

I hesitated before saying, "I got a job with an insurance company."

Jeff nodded and waited for me to continue. When I didn't, he said, "Straight commission?"

"Yeah."

"Well, we know you can sell, so that's not a worry. How long before you start making any money?"

Good question. I hadn't thought about that. It only took me one day in the car business, though, so I was pretty sure

I'd be OK. I shrugged again. "Not long, according to what they told me."

"So why do you think you'll like it better?"

"For one thing, when I make a sale I keep getting paid as long as the people keep the policy. And I don't have to sit in one place. I get to go out and find my own customers. As many as I want."

"OK." Jeff nodded. "That's fair, I guess. Think you'll get the same check next week you'd be getting here?"

Hmmm. I hadn't thought about that one either. Once again, I shrugged.

Jeff leaned his chair back and scratched his chin, staring at me the whole time. "Sounds like you've got your mind made up, but let me point out one thing. You might not see it now, but you've got a great future here. This could be your office one day." He shut up, wisely just letting his words sink in.

Yet one more thing I hadn't considered. My analytical skills weren't very good back then, I guess.

I looked around the room. Awards hung behind Jeff's desk. Others shared shelf space with thick binders and bundles of brochures on a couple of plain bookcases. One wall had a two-way mirror that allowed the sales manager to look out on the sales floor. This same office had probably been my uncle's ten years earlier.

Jeff was a great guy and excellent manager, but he wasn't going to beg me to stay. That's not how the car business works. He was giving some things to think about, though. And what he was telling me, I realized, was that this would be my ultimate goal if I stayed in the car business. Maybe not that specific office, but one just like it at another dealership.

After a few minutes Jeff leaned forward, resting his elbows on the edge of his desk. "Go home. I'll make sure any deals you've got working are covered. Take the weekend to think this thing over, then let me know on Monday morning. How's that sound?"

I nodded, but we both knew I wasn't going to change my mind. He stood and offered me his hand. As we shook, he said, "Whatever you decide, you know you've always got a place here."

I thanked him and walked away from a six-figure income. I wanted to chase my future. About halfway home I realized there was still one more thing I hadn't counted on in my rush to leave the dealership. In order to sell insurance and be paid commissions, the state of Texas requires completion of a forty-hour pre-licensing course followed by a passing score on the state licensing exam. Until I accomplished those two things, I didn't have a job.

HEATH'S TAKEAWAYS FOR SUCCESS

On Action Bias

If you wait to start life's journey until everything's ready and you know everything you'll need to know, you won't ever take the first step. The best and quickest way to learn something is by doing it. Now, if you're going to be a brain surgeon or run a nuclear power plant, you need to know exactly what you're doing before you make that first attempt on your own. Most of us are never going to attempt brain surgery, though, so it's important to act before opportunities pass by.

For most of us, the most important thing is to quit overthinking things and move forward. You can't take step number two until you take step number one. Mistakes are every bit as sure in life as death and taxes. Doing whatever it takes to avoid them guarantees that you'll one day look back on a life of fear and regrets.

Changing your life, starting a business, or chasing your dreams all take a lot of time and effort to finally get right. At some point, time spent planning, preparing, and learning is just putting you further behind. Take the first step. Then take the second one. Before you know it, you'll have stepped your way farther than you imagined.

One day you'll look back and see all the mistakes you made. It's OK to wish you had done things different. It's not OK to look back and realize you wasted your life waiting for just the right time and the perfect opportunity.

What is the single biggest fear that keeps you from taking the first step toward the thing you most want in life?

_____

_____

_____

_____

What is the worst thing that could happen when you take that step?

_____

_____

_____

_____

Is what you wrote above worse than being exactly where you are right now in twenty years? You can't take the next step until you've taken the first one!

THREE

RUNNING BACK TO MY COMFORT ZONE

A smart person would have been scared to death of failing the insurance exam and having no income. A smart person would have studied hard, then gone back and learned it all again before taking the test. *Whatever.* I'd made it through three semesters of junior college and taken the car sales world by storm. I signed up for the self-study course and the next testing date and didn't think about it again. After all, I only had to make a seventy.

On the day of the exam, I breezed into the testing center. I scored a fifty-two.

No worries. I laughed it off and signed up to try again. Instead of completely blowing off the course the second time around, I studied the parts I'd struggled with. Truthfully, that was most of them.

The second try went much better. Score? Sixty-seven.

Now the whole process had my attention. Regardless of what I'd told the general manager back at the dealership, I hadn't saved any of the money I'd made selling cars, so it was time to take this thing a little more seriously. I had a friend already covering my rent. I couldn't wait any longer to get some money coming in.

The exam textbook was one of the thickest I'd put my hands on, but I dug into it, trying to memorize words and laws and formulas and numbers. The next time I walked into the exam center, I had my game face on. The investment had been made. It was time for the payoff.

I finished the test for the third time and then waited, bouncing in my chair like a Mexican jumping bean. When my score finally flashed up on the screen, I smashed my fist into the desk and stormed out of the building.

Sixty-nine. One point short.

If I'd been playing horseshoes that would have been fine. On a state-regulated exam, a sixty-nine might as well be a zero.

My humiliation was complete. Over and over, I saw myself standing in front of Jeff, strapping my boots up and swallowing my pride, telling him he was right and begging for my job back. The taste of my own pride makes me sick.

And that's the moment I was sitting in my truck, jamming my fingers against the buttons as I dialed my phone, waiting through those long, empty rings for Mom to answer. Finally, she picked up.

"A sixty-nine. One stupid point," I said, slamming my hand against the steering wheel.

Mom's only reply was, "Well . . . " Then she went silent, letting me stew.

Through the windshield, I saw a couple of others who'd taken the exam leave the building. Both were smiling as they exchanged a high five.

"I'm never going to pass this stupid thing," I whined to Mom. "I'm going to go ahead and go back to the car dealership. At least I'm smart enough to sell cars."

"Are you sure that's what you want to do?"

"I'm too broke to take it again." I blew out a huge breath and looked up at the truck roof. "I mean, I can't ask Brandon to keep covering all the rent."

Silence from the other end of the call told me Mom had decided not to interrupt my pity party.

When I couldn't stand it anymore, I said, "Don't you think I should just go do something I'm good at? You know I'm not smart enough to pass a test like this."

I braced for another bout of quiet, but Mom must have decided we'd both suffered enough.

"You're too close to just give up. If you want to go sell cars, that's fine. Pass that test first, though. *Then* go get your old job back."

In the back of my mind, I'd been hoping she'd say, "No way. Stay away from the dealership." I'm rebellious enough that I would have felt justified running back to my comfort zone. But I should have known Mom was smarter than that.

"You don't have to decide today," she added. "At least take a little while to think things through."

I shook my head. "I can't do it. I've got to make some money."

"I know it seems bad right now," she said. "And you know we'll support you, whatever you decide. Just remember, you made a promise to the people who hired you."

That wasn't what I wanted to hear, but something about her words rang true. In fact, they made me remember something my dad taught me another time I'd tried to quit, nine years earlier. I didn't know it sitting in my truck that day, but what I learned from Dad back in the summer of 1997 was about to help me turn what could have been a life-changing failure into a huge success.

FOUR

WISDOM FROM MOM AND DAD

Have you ever spent what seemed like a long time looking forward to something, then found out it wasn't anything like you thought? The disappointment is huge, and it seems like nothing will ever be right again. That's what happened to me the summer I was ten years old.

I spent the last weeks of school thinking about nothing but hanging out with my friends and playing baseball. When it came time to sign up, though, my buddies got split up between two leagues—one in Troup and one in Carlisle. I could play for either one since we lived between the two towns, but having to choose between my buddies upset me. At least until I figured out I didn't have to choose. If I could play in *either* league, I could play in *both* leagues. Genius!

My parents disagreed. When I explained my plan, Dad sat me down for one of those father-son talks.

"That's a lot of baseball, isn't it?" he asked.

I wasn't sure how to answer. Sure it was. But it was *baseball*! The safest answer seemed to be a simple, "Yes, sir."

"You don't think you'll get tired of it?"

Tired of playing baseball with my friends? Maybe my parents weren't as smart as I thought they were. Again, I shook my head and went with the safest, most truthful answer. "No, sir."

Dad rubbed his face and tried a more direct approach. "You know you'll be playing ball every single day for six weeks, don't you? Either a practice or a game. No time off to do anything else."

I nodded. That sounded great.

"And you know you can't quit just because it's not fun anymore." A statement, not a question. Both my brother and I knew our parents expected us to always finish what we started. This was baseball; I couldn't understand why Dad was so worried.

"I won't quit." Excitement ran through me. It seemed my dad's resolve was crumbling.

He let me think about it a few more seconds, then added, "You remember what I said when your friends are at Six Flags or the lake."

"I will." I was so close to getting what I wanted, I would have agreed to a lifetime ban from Six Flags *and* the lake.

Dad shook his head.

I signed up to play in both leagues.

* * * * *

Practice started a couple of days later, and I was in summertime heaven for about a week. Then, just like Dad predicted, some of my friends went to Six Flags, and all I could think about was how much fun they were having.

"Can't I have just one day off?" I begged Dad after listening to the guys from Carlisle bragging about all the stuff they did.

Dad answered with a single word. "No."

"Just one?" I whined. "Nobody's even going to miss me. I promise!"

He gave me his dreaded dad death stare. "I don't care if they miss you or not. You said you'd be there."

I knew better than to argue, but I'm sure the expression on my face left no doubt what I was thinking.

> "Just one?" I whined. "Nobody's even going to miss me. I promise!" He gave me his dreaded dad death stare. "I don't care if they miss you or not. You said you'd be there." I knew better than to argue.

"Remember what I told you?" Dad asked.

Man! He hadn't forgotten what I'd promised. I hung my head and mumbled another "Yes, sir."

He made sure I'd gotten a full dose of that death stare before I turned away, defeated.

I finished the season with both teams.

* * * * *

One of the most common causes of failure is the habit of quitting when one is overtaken by temporary defeat. Every person is guilty of this mistake at one time or another.

An uncle of R.U. Darby was caught by the "gold fever" in the gold rush days, and he went west to dig and grow rich. He had never heard that more gold has been mined from the brains of men than has ever been taken from the earth. He staked a claim and went to work with pick and shovel. The going was hard, but his lust for gold was definite.

After weeks of labor, he was rewarded by the discovery of the shining ore. He needed machinery to bring the ore to the surface. Quietly, he covered up the mine, retraced his footsteps to his home in Williamsburg, Maryland, [and] told his relatives and a few neighbors of the "strike." They got together money for the needed machinery [and] had it shipped. The uncle and Darby went to work the mine.

The first car of ore was mined, and shipped to a smelter. The returns proved they had one of the richest mines in Colorado! A few more cars of that ore would clear the debts. Then would come the big killing in profits.

Down went the drills! Up went the hopes of Darby and Uncle! Then something happened! The vein of gold ore disappeared! They had come to the end of the rainbow, and the pot of gold was no longer there! They drilled on, desperately trying to pick up the vein again—all to no avail.

Finally, they decided to *quit*.

They sold the machinery to a junk man for a few hundred dollars and took the train back home. Some "junk men" are dumb, but not this one! He called in a mining engineer to look at the mine and do a little calculating. The engineer advised that the project had failed because the owners were not familiar with "fault lines." His calculations showed that the vein would be found *just three feet from where the Darbys had stopped drilling*! That is exactly where it was found!

The "junk man" took millions of dollars in ore from the mine because he knew enough to seek expert counsel before giving up. Most of the money which went into the machinery was procured through the efforts of R.U. Darby, who was then a very young man. The money came from his relatives and neighbors, [because of their] their faith in him. He paid back every dollar of it, although he was years in doing so.

Long afterward, Mr. Darby recouped his loss many times over, when he made the discovery that *desire* can be transmuted into gold. The discovery came after he went into the business of selling life insurance.

Remembering that he lost a huge fortune, because he stopped three feet from gold, Darby profited from the experience in his chosen work, by the simple method of saying to himself, "I stopped three feet from gold, but I will never stop because men say 'no' when I ask them to buy insurance."

Darby is one of a small group of fewer than fifty men who sell more than a million dollars in life insurance annually. He owes his "stickability" to the lesson he learned from his "quitability" in the gold mining business.

Before success comes in any man's life, he is sure to meet with much temporary defeat, and, perhaps, some failure. When defeat overtakes a man, the easiest and most logical thing to do is to *quit*. That is exactly what the majority of men do.

—From *Think and Grow Rich*, Napoleon Hill (The Napoleon Hill Foundation, original publisher, 1937; New York: Penguin Group, 2003, 2005), pp. 5, 6.

* * * * *

I'd planned to quit the team from Troup and stick with the one in Carlisle. As it turned out, Troup went on to the playoffs at the end of the regular season while the Carlisle team went home. We didn't make a deep playoff run, but it was a great experience I would have missed if Dad and Mom had given in. Six Flags and the lake wouldn't have been much fun while my friends from Troup strutted around bragging about making the playoffs.

Dad couldn't have known back then how making me keep my commitment to the Troup baseball team would change my life.

I didn't think much about it again until that day in my truck when I tried to convince Mom I had failed. Her words stung, but she reminded me who I was and what the expectations I had been raised with were.

This time, the decision whether I would follow through

was entirely mine. Thankfully, I made the right call. I had made a commitment to my new employer and to myself. It was time to keep on keeping on.

Instead of going back to the dealership that morning and begging for my job back, I went home and dug into the course material yet again. Two days later, on my fourth attempt, I finally passed the exam—seventy-one, this time—and started on an incredible journey.

It's one that has allowed me to help hundreds, if not thousands, of people achieve their dreams.

FIVE

NO PLAN B

Achieving a seemingly impossible goal is an awesome feeling. Just about everybody has walked away from that big win—whether it's making a sale, earning a good grade, or acing a job interview—feeling like the biggest, baddest superhero ever to wear a cape. For a while, life seems easier.

Passing that exam, even just barely, made me feel like I could fly. Instead of slinking back to the car dealership, I started a career I knew would let me achieve my dreams.

Or, at least, what I thought my dreams were at the time.

That first week was overwhelming, so I didn't think much more about the lesson my parents had taught me that summer of 1997. I was too busy trying to make sense of all the information my new boss wanted me to absorb.

After a week of learning products and sales techniques, I was in the field having more fun than I'd ever had at my old job. In the first month, my income was back up to the same level it had been at the car dealership. I was living the dream—until I woke up one morning and realized it had turned into a nightmare.

Making sales and getting the biggest paycheck possible took all my attention. I didn't bother learning the difference between a sale and a good sale. A sale generates a quick commission. But a *good* sale always benefits the buyer—which means it usually stays on the books and generates a steady stream of commission.

After about six weeks of being unstoppable, I couldn't close a deal to save my life. Plus, most of the bad sales I'd made started falling off the books. That meant I had to pay back all of the commissions I thought I'd earned.

> It's hard to appreciate the struggle when things are tough, but great reward is usually the result of great struggle.

Everybody goes through tough times, especially when their income is based on commissions. It's just part of life. Smart people know it, prepare for it, and adapt to it. Unfortunately, I'm not usually the smartest guy in a room. I thought I'd left the tough times behind when I got a seventy-one on that exam, so there was no reason to worry anymore. Right?

The good news: I'm a lot smarter now than I was then. The bad news: I really, *really* wasn't smart back then. Even when I wasn't closing any sales, I kept living like the money was rolling in. The problem with that, of course, is the bills still have to be paid, even when the money runs out. It didn't take long for me to lose my swagger again.

Going broke the second time was even harder because my initial success had gained a lot of attention not only from my company, but from my family and friends as well. They saw me as the local kid who did good. If failing hadn't been an option before, it really wasn't where I wanted to go once I'd gotten started.

So, just like with that test, I kept on keeping on. A typical agent in our office, selling door to door, completed six appointments each week. I *hustled*—I averaged twenty-one appointments each week, and yet I was still behind almost everybody else in sales.

I would never have admitted it then, but going back to the car dealership, at that point, was a real temptation once again. That would have been a full-blown retreat. But I also knew what kind of income I could make, and a car dealership never takes back a commission!

The sensible thing, to most people, would have been to go back to what worked and take the easy money. In fact, not walking away from a six-figure income in the first place would seem like the sensible thing to most people. Thank goodness I've never been like most people.

> Too many people approach a new opportunity with Plan B all set up, just in case. They want to dip their toes in the water and see what happens, knowing they have a safe option when— notice I said *when*, not *if*—things don't work out. If keeping on keeping on is a requirement for success, Plan B is a guarantee of failure.

Successful leaders almost all share certain traits that separate them from the crowd. Not quitting—even when honoring a commitment seems too hard, too expensive, or too time-consuming—is one of them. I resented my parents for the rest of the summer when they wouldn't let me quit on my baseball teammates. Now, I'm thankful they taught me such an important lesson while I was so young.

My parents didn't have a formal set of principles written down to raise us with. They just expected us to do the right thing, like never giving up and keeping our commitments. That meant that going back to car sales—the "smart play," some might call it—was never really an option for me.

Some weeks I barely made enough money to buy the gas I needed to get to my appointments. Still, I knew from experience that if I followed through with my training, good things would happen.

If I had just known how soon those good things would happen, I might have slept a lot better back then.

HEATH'S TAKEAWAYS FOR SUCCESS

On Mind-set

Your mind-set is everything. Like mistakes, obstacles are part of life. Mind-set determines how we deal with them. Without the proper mind-set, it's easy to feel sorry for yourself and blame others for your problems. The trouble with that reaction is you wind up with even more of what you already have. Taking responsibility for your own actions is the only way to move forward and achieve what you want.

Keeping a positive mind-set takes work. You have to train your mind to respond the way you want. Just like building confidence when you're still inexperienced, you keep your mind-set positive by reading the right books and listening to the right podcasts. With today's technology—smart phones, earbuds, Bluetooth—it's easy to keep a positive message in your ear.

A good way to keep a great mind-set is to always start your day in a positive way. Getting up thirty minutes earlier to read good, positive books will always get you moving in the right direction. If reading isn't something you enjoy, listen to an audio book or podcast to start your day. Maintaining a positive mind-set is up to you. Give yourself the tools you need to get the job done.

I've included a list of the five most powerful books I've read as a resource at the end of this book.

Do you usually see an obstacle as a threat or an opportunity?

_____

_____

_____

Besides reading this book and completing these exercises, what are you doing to maintain a growth-oriented mind-set?

_____

_____

_____

Based on what you've read in *Ignorance on Fire*, what steps can you take, starting today, toward building and maintaining a healthy mind-set?

_____

_____

_____

_____

Write down a specific situation that will have—or might have had—a better result if approached with a positive, growth-oriented mind-set.

SIX

THE SALES CALL I
ALMOST DIDN'T MAKE

A lot of people say they don't care what others think, and it's important for a leader to make decisions without fearing the opinions of others. Most of us, though, no matter how tough we want to be, worry about how family and friends see us.

Even with the rent covered, I spent every day stressing over how to pay bills. Losing my local-boy-done-good image worried me just as much.

Those fears made the temptations that come with money troubles strong. It would have been easy to cut corners in my sales presentations. Telling my prospects whatever they wanted to hear would have guaranteed some quick cash and let me concentrate on moving forward. That also would have kept up the shiny, fragile image of success I'd developed. No amount of income would have protected me from myself, though, so I kept on doing the right thing.

About three months after the bottom fell out, a lead came in for a Medicare prescription card. It wasn't even a little bit exciting because the prospect lived in Longview, more than forty miles from my office. *If* I managed to make the sale, the commission on one of those cards was only about fifty bucks. That would barely cover my gas costs.

It's hard to describe how much I wanted to just blow off that appointment. I mean, keeping on keeping on is one thing, but going all the way to Longview for the chance to earn practically nothing seemed flat-out stupid. But I'd made a commitment, so I got in the truck and headed south.

The prospect lived in a pretty nice house in an attractive neighborhood. It was a lot better than anywhere I'd ever lived, but ringing the doorbell didn't make me uncomfortable. A clean, older Dodge pickup sat in the driveway next to a gleaming new Cadillac.

The prospects, Mr. and Mrs. Brown, turned out to be an older couple, and we spent a few minutes getting acquainted around their kitchen table. As much as I'd wanted to skip the appointment, I was glad I hadn't let an excuse get the best of me. We really hit it off, and they immediately took me under their wing like I was family.

On any sales call, the first thing I did was complete a fact-finding questionnaire to learn about the potential clients and their needs. We covered things like existing insurance policies, income, investments, and potential liabilities. When I brought up annuities, Mr. Brown stood and crossed to the counter separating the kitchen and breakfast area. He picked up a large envelope, thick with papers, and slapped it down in front of me.

"What do you think of this?" he asked.

I saw the crest of a popular investment firm as I pulled

the statement from the envelope. Glancing over the top page, I froze. I'm pretty sure I didn't let my mouth hang open and my tongue flop out, but I'll never be completely certain. The account balance was more than one million dollars.

I knew enough about investments to understand that an annuity was a much better choice. I also knew enough to back up and bring in an expert. Instead of trying to impress the Browns with what I didn't know, I put the statement back in the envelope and said, "I've got some ideas, but this is going to take some research. Let's go ahead and take a look at the prescription card you asked about, and I'll come back with my manager." I pulled one of our prescription cards from my bag. "Have you got the card you're using now?"

Mr. Brown laid it on the table. After taking a look, I knew what the Browns already had was a better fit for them than our card would be. I recommended they keep it. I didn't make a sale that day, but I did earn a prospect's trust.

They agreed to meet again to look at options for annuities.

We got together five or six times over the next six weeks, and each time I learned something new about life and success. Working as a team, the Browns had done incredibly well financially, much better than their house or cars suggested. Since that was exactly what I wanted in life, I hung on every word Mr. Brown shared about his business triumphs.

His regrets weren't nearly as much fun to listen to. I didn't want to hear about any downside to achieving my dream. It was like driving by a bad car wreck or a natural disaster, though. As hard as I tried, I couldn't turn away.

This couple had everything I wanted, but they were still

humble, gracious, and grateful. I didn't understand how they could have any regrets. And yet, over the course of those few weeks, I learned that, given the chance, they wouldn't have hesitated to go back and invest their time and effort in their family instead of their business. My definition of success didn't change, but the Browns planted a seed that would lead me to question everything I thought I knew once it started to grow.

Sometimes, failing your way forward is the only way to reach the goal.

Six weeks after that first appointment, I closed the biggest sale of my life. My commission and bonus were almost as much money as I'd made in any single year. All of a sudden, I felt like I was wearing that cape again. I couldn't believe how my luck had turned.

Not keeping that first appointment had seemed like the most sensible thing to do at the time. I almost ignored the fact-finder that was supposed to be done at *every* sales call, no matter what. Making either of those decisions would have changed my life for the worse. Once again, a lesson from my past came to the rescue.

When I was twelve, my dad taught me about never giving less than 100 percent when it comes to doing a job. Ever since that day, I've always half-expected him to be lurking around the corner, ready to pounce if I failed to give someone my best effort.

SEVEN

H&J LAWN SERVICE

Growing up, I was always looking for a way to earn extra spending money. When I was twelve my best friend, Jesse, and I started our own plant business. His parents owned a nursery and gardening center, and we talked them into giving us fifteen or twenty plants on the promise we would pay them from the profits we made selling them. Before making our first sale, we took cuttings so we could grow our own inventory and keep all the money for ourselves.

We were serious about building our business, so we used some scrap lumber and plastic sheeting to build a greenhouse out in the woods. Thinking back, the result of our efforts looked more like a mess than a greenhouse, but it was something to work with. We even set up a constant watering system. We cut the bottoms out of two-liter soda bottles, hung them upside down over the plants, and filled them with water. Then, we unscrewed the caps just enough to create a continuous leak.

Every Saturday morning we'd get up early and hook a trailer to our four-wheelers, then fill them with plants and hit the road, Jesse and I heading in opposite directions. I would spend all day going door to door, trying to sell Purple Jews and ferns to any neighbor foolish enough to talk to me. Jessie and I were captains of industry . . . until a thunderstorm tore our greenhouse apart and wiped out our inventory.

When we realized that we still had to pay Jessie's parents for the plants, we figured it was time to find a money-making venture that didn't need things like insurance and emergency cash funds. Later that day, we both commandeered our families' lawnmowers and established H&J Lawn Service.

Most of the yards out where I grew up are large—at least an acre. If you've ever push-mowed that much grass, you know it's a big job. Even so, every morn-

> "A setback is a setup for a comeback."[1]
> — Les Brown

ing in the summer, Jessie and I hooked our trailers up to our four-wheelers, loaded the equipment, and prowled the roads searching for yards that needed our attention.

My parents always encouraged both my brother and me in our money-making adventures. We just had to always keep Dad's one hard-and-fast rule. Early on, he told both of us that Oakes was his name before it was ours, so everything we did reflected back on him. When we made ourselves look bad, he said, we made him look even worse.

The rule was that we always had to follow through on our commitments and always give 100 percent effort to any job we did. Without being told, my brother and I knew breaking that rule would make for a really, really bad day. What we didn't know was that Dad constantly checked up on us.

Jessie and I had a pretty good gig going, but *enough* wasn't a word in my vocabulary. I wanted more money, so we had to increase our workload. That meant putting more effort into doing our jobs fast than we put into doing them well.

Dad came home one evening while I was unloading my trailer, and I knew from the look on his face that trouble had found me. I mean trouble with a capital T. Before I could speak, he jerked his head back toward his truck and said, "Get in."

The only thing I wanted to do less than get in that truck with my dad right then was argue with him. So I tried to dodge the whole thing. I lifted my gas can from the trailer.

"I've got to get this equipment put up."

"Leave it."

I still didn't know what was going on, but I had a sudden feeling this might turn out even worse than I thought.

I put the can down and headed for the truck. That's when Dad hit me with the full force of his death stare. My thoughts raced, trying to figure out what I'd done, but nothing came to mind. Instead of giving me any clues, Dad drove with one hand draped across the top of the wheel, eyes straight ahead, jaw clenched.

After what seemed like a hundred miles, we stopped in front of a house where Jessie and I had been earlier that morning. He put the truck in park and asked, "Did you cut this yard?"

"Yes, sir," I answered without even looking.

"Did you do a good job?"

I squirmed in my seat. "Yeah. I mean, Jessie and me got it all cut."

Dad turned and looked at me, eyebrows raised. "*All* of it? You *sure?*"

"Yes, sir."

Then I looked out the window, and my stomach fell to my tennis shoes. All across this neighbor's yard, strips of neatly cut grass alternated with rows of ankle-high weeds. There was no getting around it: the yard looked terrible.

I hadn't just broken Dad's hard-and-fast rule. I'd thrown it on the ground and smashed it into a hundred pieces. Needless to say, the conversation my dad and I had in the truck that afternoon wasn't pretty, so I won't share the details. I'll just say he made it clear that I had failed to protect his name and I was going to correct my mistake.

Arguing with Dad was never a good idea, especially when he had "that look," but this was serious business. I took a deep breath and stepped onto some very thin ice.

"But Jessie helped," I said. "Shouldn't we go get him, too?"

"His last name Oakes?" Dad demanded.

"No, sir."

"Then don't worry about him."

Man, this was so unfair! I knew better than to push it, though. While Dad waited, I hoofed it back to our house, fired up the ATV, and drove back with my lawnmower in tow. It didn't seem like too big a job. I mean, at least half the grass was already cut, and it wasn't hard to find what I'd missed. I gassed the mower up, yanked the pull cord, and started on the nearest swath of weeds.

Dad, however, had a different view of things.

He waved at me to cut the engine, shook his head, and said, "Do the whole yard. Not just what you missed."

That was the stupidest thing I'd ever heard! It was late and I was tired. No way I wanted to mow grass that had already been cut. I opened my mouth to protest, but Dad's fierce scowl killed the words while they were still in the back of my throat. I grabbed the pull cord and yanked the engine back to life and got to work. Dad crossed the road and leaned against the truck, arms crossed, watching me like a hawk. *This is the worst day ever,* I told myself over and over as I mowed.

When I finally finished—again!—Dad walked around the yard inspecting my work while I got the equipment loaded back on the trailer. I climbed on my four-wheeler, glad this day was finally finished. Except . . . it wasn't.

I nearly fell off my seat when Dad said, "Not so fast. How much did he pay you?"

"Twenty dollars."

"You still got it?"

I nodded. This conversation was going south in a hurry.

Dad jerked his head toward the house. "Go give his money back and apologize."

I couldn't believe what I'd just heard. Summertime in East Texas is hot, and I'd cut a bunch of yards that day. One of them twice. Now my dad wanted me to work for free!

When I didn't move fast enough, he added, "You made a promise. You didn't keep it."

He had a point, but right then that yard looked a lot better than just twenty bucks.

Dad took a half step in my direction. "I'm not going to tell you again."

I could feel his stare burning into my back as I drug my feet all the way to our neighbor's front steps, putting this humiliation off as long as I could. The man accepted my apology with good humor and allowed me to refund his money. When we were done, he shook my hand, then looked up and gave my dad a wink. I'm happy to say he stayed a regular customer for the rest of that summer.

If I had just given it a 100 percent effort the first time, I could have been hanging out with my friends instead of trying to fix a broken promise. Even better, I would have had more money in my pocket. Remembering that day as an adult, I realized it was my dad who kept me doing the right thing when my sales collapsed, even though it would have been easier to feel sorry for myself and just coast.

> If I had just given it a 100 percent effort the first time, I could have been hanging out with my friends instead of trying to fix a broken promise. Even better, I would have had more money in my pocket. Remembering that day as an adult, I realized it was my dad who kept me doing the right thing when my sales collapsed.

I'm not saying I didn't have my share of self-pity when I had to depend on friends to make ends meet. I promise you, I did. And you would know I wasn't being honest if I said I threw myself into my work every minute of every day. But because of what my dad taught me about giving my best effort—even when no one is looking and no results are guaranteed—it always just seemed like the best option.

Still, I sometimes look over my shoulder—even today—just to make sure my dad's not behind me, ready to make me do a job all over again if I try to cut a corner . . . or cut a yard poorly.

He wouldn't have said this, but in Troup, Texas the shoddy work Dad called me out on is referred to as half-assed. Not long ago, I was remembering that incident and the lesson I learned from it, and I got to wondering where that phrase originated. I thought it was just an East Texas redneck saying, but that's not the case at all. It actually has a pretty interesting history that ties in with what my Dad taught me about always giving 100 percent.

EIGHT

A HALF-ADZED JOB

Back in the days before electric tools, lumber had to be planed and shaped by hand before it could be used for things like cabinets, flooring, or in the case of the title of this chapter, fireplace mantles. (What "a half-adzed job" means will make sense in just a few lines!) To make the wood usable, carpenters used a tool called an adze, an instrument still used by craftsmen today.

An adze has a handle similar to an ax. The steel head bends into a sharp, horizontal blade like a duck's bill, curving down. Back in the 1700s, wealthy families who built a house would pay extra to have their fireplace mantles shaped and smoothed on all sides—even the back part that no one could see. Poorer or thriftier families spent less money by having only the top half of the mantle finished. That meant they got a "half-adzed job."

Now, delivering a half-adzed mantle wouldn't necessarily reflect poorly on the carpenter. As long as he put 100 percent effort into the job, he delivered exactly what the customer paid for. Everybody knows how tempting it is, though, to slack off a little when we're given a small task that probably won't yield big results. Who's going to see the back of the mantle, anyway?

In the case of the carpenter, a poor family would never create repeat business, so it probably seemed easy to give that family less value for its money. I've never used an adze or any of the tools woodworkers used back then, but my guess is it took just as much time and effort to set the shop up for a half-finished mantle as it did for one getting a full-adzed job. So, no doubt, it would have been easy—even tempting—for the carpenter to hurry through the work so he could either complete more jobs (sound familiar?) or move on to something more profitable.

A good leader understands that even minimum jobs deserve maximum effort, and he or she will inspire others to the same belief. Most of us have heard the saying, "Any job worth doing is worth doing well." Yes, it's a cliché, but the reason a saying turns into a cliché usually is because it's true and deserves repeating. Just like this one. The day my dad made me recut our neighbor's lawn would have turned out a lot better for me if I'd heard this particular cliché more often.

So many people think it's easier to just slide by—whether it's in their jobs, their relationships, or their other commitments. They don't invest anything more into a task than they think they will get out of it. That might sound like a good plan at first, but it winds up costing more in time, money, and reputation than it would have cost to give 100 percent effort the first time around.

* * * * *

It took several years for me to figure out how my dad's lesson that day guided me through the first years of my professional life. I assumed my early success was due to luck, but luck isn't something you can count on. The idea of my "luck running out" one day terrified me. I won't say I haven't had some good fortune, but giving a full effort always pays off. It might not be in the way we want, or in the time frame we expect, but it's something we can always count on.

It's been said, "Luck is what happens when preparation meets opportunity." How many times do people miss out on achieving their goals and living their dreams because they aren't ready when the opportunity comes along? Instead of giving 100 percent, they base their effort on the expected return. When opportunity presents itself, that kind of effort isn't usually strong enough to let them grab on and fly.

After the stock market took a nose dive in 2008, I went back to see the Browns. Mr. Brown had taken a lot of ribbing from his friends about moving his investments to an annuity. Had they not made the switch, however, the Browns would have lost a huge amount of money. They couldn't thank me enough for helping them avoid that.

It was the first time I suspected that helping people and being successful might just be the same thing.

NINE

DINNER MEETING

With a big payday from my annuity sale, it didn't take long to get my life back on track. Money rolled in again, and I was making progress toward achieving what, at the time, I thought were my dreams. My job was fun and the company I worked for a good one. I was pretty impressed with the choices I'd made.

A few weeks later, a recruiter from another insurance company called. I hadn't thought about making a change, but I never say no to something until I know what it is I'm saying no to. I kind of halfway listened to what the guy said. Then, somewhere in all those words he was throwing at me, I heard, "How would you like to have your own insurance agency?"

That got my attention, but it sounded kind of out there at the same time.

Instead of letting him know how much I liked the idea, I laughed and said something like, "But I don't know what the heck I'm doing. I've only been in this business for a few months."

"You don't have to worry about that," he told me. "We'll set you up and train you to be the best agency owner in the business."

"You do know I'm only nineteen years old, don't you?" I asked.

"That's great. We can get you started working the right way before you learn too many bad habits."

I was pretty naïve, but I knew enough to slow down and look at this thing carefully. I also knew, even then, that when something sounds too good to be true, it usually is. But this guy on the phone said he'd like to talk with me in person. Again, I wanted to know exactly what I would be saying no to, so I agreed to meet him for supper in Dallas.

I knew it would be a nicer meal than I was used to. When I wanted a good steak—I mean, when I was ready to throw some cash down for a fine meal—Outback Steakhouse was my go-to spot. Something a little more upscale was the expectation I had when I put on one of my two seventy-two-dollar suits and hopped in my truck.

That pickup was my pride and joy. It was a black F250 with a seven-inch lift, twenty-two-inch wheels, and thirty-seven-inch tires. If you're not from Texas, all of that means it was a young redneck's dream. A huge, perfect vehicle for East Texas. It was something altogether different when I rolled into Dallas traffic for only the second time in my life. I must have been a real spectacle on I-635, black smoke rolling behind me while I cut people off in all six lanes.

My perspective on the world and my place in it changed

as soon as I pulled up to III Forks Steakhouse and Seafood Restaurant. The first thing I did was try to go around the parking valet. It wasn't just the money; I didn't trust *anybody* with my truck. Valet parking was the only option available, though, so I got out and let some guy I'd never seen before have my baby.

Looking around, I knew from my time selling cars that I was in a place I'd only dreamed about. Compared to the high-dollar luxury cars that filled the parking lot, my truck seemed totally out of place. A couple of minutes later, the valet came back and said the thing was too big for him to maneuver. He told me to go ahead park it myself. Yep, this meeting was off to a great start!

The recruiter and I met at the bar, and he told me to order whatever I wanted. The place was pretty intimidating, but I put on my manliest expression and ordered what I thought I could get away with. My plan wasn't real clear, but looking around, I vowed to make myself a part of this new world.

Once my new friend—we'll call him Mr. Smith—and I were seated, I almost fell out of my chair when I opened the menu. The prices were unbelievable! It took a lot of effort to keep my mouth from flopping open. I found myself clueless when Mr. Smith asked, "So what looks good to you?"

Thankfully, a coherent thought made its way through my brain and down to my mouth. Instead of just shaking my head, I managed to say, "What would you get?"

It shouldn't have been a surprise when he pointed out the bone-in ribeye—the most expensive choice on the menu. While I ate the best steak I'd ever had, Mr. Smith laid out a plan I could use to launch my own business. It would take a lot of hard work, but I always figured that would be part of the deal.

What he showed me looked a lot like the stuff my dreams were made of.

I had no idea how much those dreams would change during the journey I was about to begin.

TEN

OAKES INSURANCE AGENCY ...
BUT SOMETHING'S NOT RIGHT

Oakes Insurance Agency opened its door for the first time in April 2008. The fact that the actual agency door led into the apartment I shared with a friend of mine didn't make it any less awesome to me.

Mr. Smith had left his corporate job and established his own general agency. He would be responsible for training me and two other new agency owners. That should have been a red flag, but I was too excited about working with somebody who had achieved so much success to notice my mistake.

One thing he insisted I do from the start was hold regular Monday morning meetings with my agents. On that first day, I only had one. Paul went to work at the car dealership about a month after I did, and we'd become good friends. He sat on the edge of my bed during that first meeting. You read that right: he sat on my bed for that first meeting!

Another thing I learned early was that the lifeblood of any insurance agency is new agents. In order to stay in business, a manager must constantly be on the lookout for good talent. I took that lesson to heart, and it wasn't long before we saw a lot more people at our Monday meetings.

I knew at the start it would be a challenge getting an agency off the ground, but I didn't know how much effort it would take. We worked our butts off. In addition to selling the products, I was responsible for recruiting new agents and teaching them how to do our business. I got some training from the companies we represented, but the best way for me to learn something has always been to do it, screw it up, and keep doing it over again until I get it right. I've made an art form of failing my way to success. Getting the right people in place was no different.

Hiring new agents was just the start of the process. Once they passed their state exam (I know you remember *that* story!), got licensed, and signed a contract, it was up to me to train them. At this point, me training somebody was kind of like a man with his eyes closed leading a blind man by the hand. We made a lot of good sales, but we missed plenty as well. Still, we were posting good numbers and getting better at our jobs every day.

In spite of ourselves, the business grew. Within two months we had moved out of my apartment into a two-room office in Tyler. Our new space was tiny, and we weren't there long, but that little office building will always be a special place for me. While we were moving in, I found a box in one of the closets. It contained two books, *The 21 Irrefutable Laws of Leadership* by John Maxwell and *See You at the Top* by Zig Ziglar. (These are on my list of must-read recommendations at the end of this book.)

In high school I did anything—and I mean *anything*—to avoid reading. I had never read an entire book in my life. Both those titles caught my attention, though, so I put them in my bookcase before I threw the box out. My shelves are a little nicer now, but I still have those same two books in my office today.

Within two months the agency moved again, and it was a big step up. We were in our own building. A large sign over the front door said Oakes Insurance Agency. I have to say, I thought I was somebody! My dad was happy for me, and proud, but he was still Dad. I found him outside one day, staring at the front of the building. I stepped beside him, and he pointed at the sign.

"You see that name up there?" he asked.

I looked at him to make sure he was serious, then said, "Yes, sir."

"It's my name, too. You screw up, you make me look bad. Don't forget that."

"I promise," I said with a laugh. The day I spent recutting our neighbor's yard ten years earlier was still fresh in my mind, so Dad had nothing to worry about.

One thing that drove me to push myself and my agents so hard was competition. Mr. Smith had set up his office in Dallas, and I traveled there for a meeting every couple of weeks. At the first one, I met the other two agency owners

Mr. Smith had hired.

Both were a little older than me, and both were really good at sales. We shook hands that first time—and then it was on. They seemed like good guys, but no way were they going to out-produce me! The competition was both fierce and fun. I usually won.

Other than competition, the thing that drove me was money. I saw everything I'd ever wanted when I looked at Smith and his lifestyle. He didn't only know what to order at the best restaurants, he wore expensive clothes and had opened a nice office. He drove a new Mercedes S550 and lived in a beautiful McMansion. He had the money to enjoy his life. Deep down, I knew that if this guy could make it, I could too.

Hard work can be exhilarating, especially when you see yourself getting closer to your dreams. Putting in the hours and watching your future disappear over the horizon, however, can be soul-crushing. Each week Mr. Smith was at the top of the company reports even though he never sold a policy. The only place the three of us who reported to him saw our names was in his personal newsletter.

Something was beginning to smell bad.

With all our sales, my agents and I should have been doing well. In fact, according to the plan Mr. Smith showed me during our dinner at III Forks, every one of us should have been making more money than we could spend by that point. Instead, we were all struggling to pay our bills. No matter how much effort we put into building our businesses, the money always seemed just out of reach.

I might have lacked business experience, but I knew enough to understand something wasn't right. It was time to start checking some things out.

HEATH'S TAKEAWAYS FOR SUCCESS

On Confidence

Most people think confidence comes from a lack of fear. That's simply not true. Confidence is knowing that you have the *competence* to handle whatever you're going to deal with today. Competence comes from doing a task, failing at it, learning from mistakes, and pursuing that same task again until you get it right. So how does someone who's young or inexperienced gain the confidence they need to move forward?

The best way I've found to develop confidence early, and to stay motivated in the face of overwhelming odds, is reading books and listening to podcasts with a positive message. (Be sure to see my list of favorite podcasts in the resource section in the back of this book.) Zig Ziglar says that what goes in your ears is what comes out of your mouth. My perspective on life and my place in it changed almost immediately when I started reading books by Mr. Ziglar, John Maxwell, and others.

Reading the success stories of others made me realize that everyone struggles in life. Why would I think I'm too special to avoid it? If you're discouraged right now because your struggles seem too hard, remember that no one lives their dreams without overcoming what appear to be impossible obstacles. People achieve their goals every single day. You can too.

List the biggest struggles you've faced at any point in your life.

_____

_____

_____

_____

_____

_____

_____

_____

_____

Now, go back and write down what came *after* the struggle. What did you learn? How did you grow? How would your life be different without each of those obstacles? How did each one affect your confidence?

_____

_____

_____

_____

_____

_____

What obstacles are you facing right now that are shaking your confidence?

_____

_____

_____

_____

_____

Go back and write down ways to resolve these struggles so they build your confidence and have a positive impact on your life today and in the future.

ELEVEN

COULD IT GET ANY WORSE?

Life would be a lot easier if it came with a pair of magic glasses that allowed us to see through the masks people wear. Life is easier, too, when we look past what we want to see and focus on who someone really is. I was so hypnotized by the things that made up Mr. Smith's image that I didn't pay attention to his intentions from the start. I believe I would have seen them if I'd looked hard enough under the surface.

Smith himself seemed like the best place to start when I tried to find out why we weren't making any money. His answer, of course, was that we just needed to work harder. I responded by saying we were already working our butts off and not getting paid for the effort. He didn't have anything else to say, and I was even more frustrated after that conversation. I believe in confronting someone directly when I have a problem with them, and I'd given him the chance to set things right.

The next step was to approach each of the different insurance companies my agency represented. I tried to stay under the radar, but someone must have said something to Mr. Smith. He called pretty quickly after I started snooping around.

"Let's get together," he told me. "I've got something you need to see."

My first instinct was to refuse. Instead, I said, "I don't have time to go to Dallas. I'm trying to work harder so I can make more money."

"I'll go to your office, then. That's part of what I want to talk about."

"Well, come on," I snapped. "I don't guess I can stop you."

He pulled into my parking lot almost exactly two hours after we ended the call. I opened the door and waved him to a chair.

"What did you want to talk about?" I asked, not exactly in my most mannered voice.

Deep inside, it was a shock to realize the starched shirt, gold cufflinks, and Allen Edmonds shoes weren't so impressive anymore. They made me wonder what was really behind the glitz.

Smith crossed his legs and straightened the crease in his pant leg, then moved right into his pitch. "It seems we've got a problem, and I think I've found a way to deal with it."

"Yeah, we do." I wasn't in a listening mood. "You put all of us on the crappiest contract we could get so you can make more money."

A lot of people would have gotten mad at my combative tone, but Smith was too smooth for that. Unlike me, he knew that, when you're mad, all that really happens is you quit listening and learning and get stupid.

"Slow down, now," he said, raising his hand like a traffic cop. "I know you're not making enough money, and I've been working with these companies to get that fixed."

If I hadn't trusted this guy before, I was done with him at that point. I stayed quiet, waiting to see what came next.

"They've only got a couple of commission levels available," he continued, "so there's no way for them to change how you're getting paid."

"You're telling me everybody who sells insurance gets paid like this?" I demanded.

"No, that's not what I said." He leaned forward and lowered his voice just a little, like we were partners in a conspiracy. "What we need to do is have everybody's commissions paid to the general agency, then I can pay y'all according to the levels we come up with."

"You mean we let you get paid for everything we do and just trust you to share it with us?"

He shrugged. "That's not how I would put it, but that's the way we get you up to the income level where you need to be."

Right away I saw his story had a pretty big hole in it, and I pounced. "Then why didn't you do that to start with?"

"My fault." He shook his head. "I didn't know how bad these contracts were. But if we go ahead and set this up, we'll have that bank account looking good in no time."

I didn't even take time to think about it. "I'm telling you right now: there's no way that's ever going to happen."

"Just think it over," he said. "I'm only trying to make sure you get what you deserve."

I stood so fast my chair spun and nearly fell over. My head buzzed with anger and I really wanted to rip into this guy. Instead, I clenched my teeth and said, "We're done here, and the best thing is for you to stay out of Tyler and me to stay away from Dallas. You need to have as little to do with me as possible."

If I had known then what was really going on, I'm not sure I could have kept such tight control. When I had first approached the companies we represented to find out why our commissions were so low, they hesitated to tell me what was going on since Smith held the master contracts. But I wouldn't take no for an answer. I wasn't exactly scrounging under the sofa cushions for gas money at that point, but nothing was left once I covered business expenses and household bills. No way I was going back to where I'd been before that big annuity sale came through.

Of course, what I didn't think about back then was that I should have saved some of the money I made when things were good. That would have made life a lot easier when the rough times came back around. Even worse, I hadn't taught my agents to save anything when commissions were high. That meant they were struggling at least as much as I was, some of them more.

When I explained my frustration to our representative at the company we did the most business with, he gave in and told me what was going on. It turned out I was right all along. They had plenty of commission structures to work with, and we were on the worst one. Based on the sales my team generated, we should have been earning at least twice as much money.

The more I learned, the madder I got.

And then, unbelievably, things got worse. The next time payday rolled around, everybody on my team—including me—got a nasty surprise. Instead of getting too little money, as expected, we got nothing.

I was looking for an eight-thousand-dollar commission

check that month. Once again, I couldn't even cover expenses. Plus, my agents had their own needs that weren't being met. They looked to me for answers, but I couldn't help them.

I could barely help myself.

TWELVE

WHAT'S THAT LIGHT AT THE END OF THE TUNNEL?

Sometimes you see light at the end of a tunnel and breathe a sigh of relief. Other times, you realize the light is actually a train barreling along at full speed and you're only halfway to the other end. You see the disaster coming. It's shaking the walls and filling the air with its exhaust, and there's exactly nothing you can do to stop it.

That's what it felt like watching my agents scramble to cover their lost income.

Ideally, the companies that owed us money would have apologized for their mistakes and forwarded our checks by overnight mail. Instead, each one told me that our commissions had been paid to Mr. Smith. He would have to answer my questions, they said. I wanted to know how that could happen without my authorization, and the guy on the phone told me I had signed an amended contract agreeing to the change. That was exactly what I had refused to do at our last meeting!

I'm not sure I've ever been as mad as I was right then. This man, who I'd believed in and depended on, had violated my trust. Because of him, I couldn't follow through with the promises I'd made to the people I'd hired. It's not hard to imagine how a hotheaded young man from East Texas wanted to handle things.

Instead, I called a lawyer.

During our first meeting, he asked me a lot of questions about what had happened and what I expected him to do.

I'm pretty sure I looked at him like he'd lost his mind as I said, "I want my eight thousand dollars!"

He smiled and told me to let him look into some things first. We agreed to meet again when he was done. I told him not to waste any time because I was broke. That seemed to amuse the attorney a lot more than it did me. A few days later he called to tell me he had some information; we set an appointment for the next morning.

> No matter what people say, perception isn't always reality. Character is.

He jumped right in when I got to his office.

"How much do you know about this guy?" he asked.

I shrugged. "Just what I've told you."

"Well." He leaned back and fixed me with a sad stare. "You certainly have a good case."

"So we're going to sue him?"

My lawyer nodded. "Sure. We can sue him for everything he's got. Which is absolutely nothing."

I laughed, literally, out loud. "Did you investigate the right guy?"

He nodded again.

"You're nuts," I said. "Mr. Smith has a new Mercedes S550, and he lives in a huge house, and he's got all these expensive clothes and a hot wife. Are you sure we're talking about the same guy?"

"Oh yeah." The lawyer sat forward and pushed a stack of papers across his desk. "Take a look. The car is rented. So is the house. The clothes probably came from a thrift shop. I can't explain the wife."

"So what do I do now?" I asked.

"Like I said . . . " He spoke slowly, as if to a child. "We can sue him if you want to, but it's going to be a big waste of your money. Even if we win, and we probably would, you'll never get anything."

I shook my head like an old dog trying to shoo away a bunch of flies. "This can't be right."

"You can't take what the man doesn't have. He's not much better off than you are right now."

I felt like I'd been punched in the gut. My "mentor" was a complete sham. The possibility had never occurred to me, and it took a while to wrap my brain around the whole thing. The money was gone. On top of that, it would take a lot of expensive and time-consuming legal work to straighten things out. I would have to prove the signature on the form assigning my team's commissions to Mr. Smith was a fake. Just like Smith himself.

None of us could wait that long to get paid. Most of my people went looking for a job while I reviewed my options. Only one choice made any sense.

THIRTEEN

SCRAMBLING . . . FOR ANYTHING

Change is a scary thing for anybody. Even the worst situation can look pretty good compared to something new and unknown. I read somewhere that it's a holdover from our ancestors, who spent every day fighting to survive in a hostile world. Leaders have to ignore that primal fear and blaze a trail into the heart of whatever waits outside the comfort zone.

Ideally, that journey begins after careful thought and deliberation. These are skills I've picked up along the way, especially when a decision affects the people I'm responsible for. When the disaster with Mr. Smith happened, however, they were qualities I still needed to learn.

Searching for a new company to represent should have terrified me, and if I had understood how little I knew about what I was doing, it probably would have. Instead,

I was just plain mad as hell. I hadn't only failed myself, I'd failed the people I'd promised to look out for. It was like somebody had dropped a bomb right in the middle of my comfort zone. I was in the last place I wanted to be.

> A leader always takes responsibility for what goes wrong on his or her watch. It's so much easier to pick up the pieces and move forward when you're not wasting time pointing fingers at someone else.

The company I first worked for took care of all the paperwork once I passed my insurance exam. I wasn't even aware of all the steps involved. Then Mr. Smith, as a managing general agent, handled everything. Letting him do the office work so I could spend time in the field training new agents and selling new business seemed like a good idea at the time. It turned out to be a really bad one, since that's what allowed him to take my team's money.

* * * * * * *

Colonial Life & Accident Insurance Company was a business I had heard Mr. Smith mention, but he didn't represent them. That made them a company I wanted to look at. Their reviews were good when I Googled them, so I figured out who I needed to talk to and gave the company a call.

When the customer service rep who answered asked how she could help, I told her I needed to speak to the vice president for sales. The silence dragged on for so long I thought we'd been cut off.

Finally, she cleared her throat and said, "Sir, are you a

policyholder or an agent?"

I didn't see why that was any of her concern, and I certainly didn't have time to chat with a phone rep. But I reasoned I would probably get better results by being nice. Instead of snapping at her, I said, "I'm a broker, and I want to sell your products. I need a contract sent to me so I can get to work."

This was my first time dealing directly with a company, but I was pretty sure Mr. Smith had handled things in a similar way when he set up my agency. It never occurred to me that, in addition to selling products I'd never heard of, this company might have a different corporate structure than what I knew. Without realizing it, I had asked for one of the company's top executives. He was responsible for every one of their ten thousand agents and sales managers.

I was too frustrated at how long this was taking to worry about any of that, though.

"OK, sir," the phone rep said. "Tell me your name and number, and I'll have our Dallas territory recruiter contact you to set an appointment."

That did it. I forgot all about getting better results by being nice.

"I want a contract," I growled. "I don't want to sit down with anybody and talk about it. I just want to get to work. Now, will you please connect me to the person who can make that happen?"

"That's what I'm trying to do, sir," the woman said, no doubt, by this time biting her tongue. "Tell me your name and give me your phone number. I'll have that person contact you as soon as she can."

"The other companies I've sold for just send out a contract and that's it. If I've got questions, I call them."

"I'm sorry." She sounded like she really was. "That's not

how we work. Let me have our Dallas recruiter contact you—I promise it will be soon—and she can get you started. I know it's not what you're used to, but you'll actually get off to a better start if you'll just follow our system. Now, what's your name and number?"

I think I kicked the trash can under my desk before I jumped up and stomped around the office, silently fuming. My first instinct was to hang up and figure out something else. This lady was good, though. Something about her voice made me believe she really wanted to help.

So, instead of once again demanding a sales contract from the number three executive in a billion-plus-dollar corporation, I gave her the information and agreed to wait for a call from the Dallas recruiter. I couldn't believe the words that came from my mouth as I thanked her and ended the call. I didn't really expect to hear from anybody, but I had told that nice lady on the phone I would wait.

Waiting: not exactly one of my strong suits.

One day, I told myself. *If nobody calls in the next twenty-four hours, I am done with these people.*

FOURTEEN

WHEN IGNORANCE AND WISDOM COLLIDE

Waiting is hard. Waiting for the solution to a big, messy problem is even worse. Being angry and unsure about the future during the wait makes it almost unbearable, especially for somebody as impatient as I am.

In this case, my worry was wasted. I heard from a local Colonial Life field manager the next morning. We agreed to meet Monday of the next week—not quickly enough for me, but that's what she could do, she said.

I got to the office early that Monday morning, ready to get things done. And . . . no one showed up. No phone call, no email. No meeting. When the territory recruiter called to follow up, I intended to tell her I was done. Somehow, though, she convinced me to accept her apology on behalf of the absent field manager and to let her make the two-hour drive from Dallas so she and I could meet.

I still hadn't done any research on the company other

than looking up their corporate contact information and reviews. When the recruiter got there, however, I was ready to sign the contract and get started. This lady had other ideas. After apologizing again for the missed meeting, she pulled out her computer and opened a PowerPoint presentation. This was not what I wanted when I agreed to see her.

"I'm sure you've got a great dog and pony show," I told her. "But I need to be out making calls this afternoon. If you want to go over the contract with me, that's fine, but I don't care about all this stuff right now." I flipped my hand at her computer like I was sweeping it away.

"I'm sorry, Heath. This is how we do things. I can't bring you on board until you've seen this presentation and gone through the process."

I thought my head was going to explode! And once she got started, it didn't take long for me to see this was an even bigger waste of time than I thought it would be. Finally, I stopped her.

When she tried to keep going, I said, "Listen, I've got eight agents I'm responsible for, and sitting here listening to you tell me a bunch of stuff I don't want to know isn't getting any of us out making money." I stood. "Thanks for coming, but you're holding me back at this point."

She didn't stand with me. Instead, she pointed to her computer and said, "Well, let me finish before you make a decision."

I glared at her, and she finally got the point and packed her things up. I watched as she pulled out onto the highway. My only thought was: *Forget these people.* But I had no idea how persistent she would be. Despite my impatience and snarkiness, she went back to her territory sales manager and told him he should give me a call.

His name was Dave Moskowitz, and when he got me on

the phone, I told him exactly how I felt.

Fortunately, Dave had been around a while and knew how to handle a guy like me. When reason, persuasion, and just plain being nice didn't work, he told me he was coming to my office. Whether or not I saw him, he said, would be up to me. *That doesn't make him look too smart,* I thought. Still, it didn't seem right to turn him away if he was willing to make that drive.

* * * * * * *

Dave pulled up in a black Mercedes almost exactly like the one Smith drove. He looked to be a little older than Smith, but he wore the same kind of clothes. Well, maybe a little nicer. Actually, Dave's clothes were tailored for him instead of being thrift shop finds, but I didn't know that then. He introduced himself and shook my hand like we were old friends. My defenses stayed up.

The things that had impressed me about Smith now proved to be two and a half strikes against Dave and his company. Trusting these people to get me out making money would have been a challenge at that point. I had agreed to see Dave. I hadn't agreed to be nice to him.

Usually when I sit down with somebody, I take the chair next to them instead of the big one behind my desk. For that first meeting, I wanted to make sure Dave understood how high the barrier was between us, so I made an exception. If I had known more about negotiation skills then, I probably would have left just one chair in front of my desk and sawed a couple of inches off the legs before he got there. I guess my ignorance worked in my favor that day. Dave had barely settled into his seat when I pounced.

"You understand you're just wasting your time, don't

you?"

"Hey, I just appreciate you seeing me. Are those your parents?" He nodded toward the picture of Mom and Dad sitting on the bookshelf behind my desk.

I shook my head. *Huh? Who was this guy?*

After a pause, I said, "Yeah. You know, I'm looking for a company I can work with, but y'all just keep yanking my chain. I don't see how you're going to change my mind."

Dave looked around my office a few moments, then cocked his head in my direction. "Have you always lived in East Texas?"

Damn it, I was mad, and I wanted a fight! He wasn't following the script I'd laid out in my mind. I decided to try my pissed-off redneck stare instead of answering. That always worked.

He responded to my fiercest scowl by asking, "Where'd you grow up?"

This guy couldn't be for real! Without softening my look, I said, "Troup."

Dave furrowed his brow. "Is that close by?"

"That way." I jerked my thumb in a southeasterly direction.

"Is all your family there?"

"Yeah." I leaned back and crossed my arms. If this guy wanted to play old home week, it was his time to waste.

"Are you married?" He crossed his legs and rested his hands on his knee.

I laughed.

Dave glanced around the office again. "Any hot prospects?"

"Not for getting married." I had to remind myself that he was the enemy to keep from saying more.

His smile faded as he put his elbows on the edge of my

desk and locked his gaze on me. "I understand you've had some bad experiences. Tell me what you need to get yourself back on track."

Ha! *That* was the opening I'd been waiting for! "What I need is a company that's going to help me sell their policies and take care of these people I hired. Y'all seem like you're more interested in slideshows and paperwork." I'd meant to be a lot nastier, but family is a big deal in East Texas—and Dave had brought my family into this. (Smart man.) It's hard to stay mad at somebody who has a real interest in your mama.

"If I remember right," Dave said, leaning back and crossing his legs again, "you've got eight agents working?"

"Well, I did a week ago. A couple have already found a job somewhere else."

"I'm sorry to hear that. Here's what we can do." He laced his fingers together and rested his hands on his knee once again. (*Relaxed guy!*, I was thinking by this point.) "I can put you on a contract that lets you and your people start making money right now."

Hmm. I had planned on kicking this bum out of my office. But Dave wasn't the monster I'd created in my mind. He was the first manager I'd talked to in this industry who made me believe he was just as concerned about my team's success as he was about his own. To Smith, we had been nothing more than a way for him to collect a nice paycheck.

Good leaders know the best investment they can make is in their people. Plenty has been written on the subject. Dave Moskowitz was a living leadership book.

I signed my name to a contract saying I'd manage people I hadn't yet recruited, selling products I hadn't yet heard of, and for a company I knew almost nothing about, all because Dave Moskowitz convinced me, without ever coming

> Dave convinced me, without ever coming out and saying it, that he cared about my success. He never tried to define exactly what success would be for me, but he left no doubt he would do all he could to help me achieve it.

out and saying it, that he cared about my success. He never tried to define exactly what success would be for me, but he left no doubt he would do all he could to help me achieve it.

Beyond my being able to get back to work and make things right, meeting with Dave that day didn't seem like a big deal at the time. In hindsight, it was my first professional exposure to real leadership. That meeting changed the course of my life.

FIFTEEN

IN SPITE OF OURSELVES

Bad things happen to everyone. Sometimes the reasons are beyond our control. More often than not, though, it's because of our own carelessness or lack of planning. Regardless, most of us spend a lot of time wondering why bad things happen, then start looking for someone to blame. Being a leader means putting the fear and anger aside, accepting responsibility, and moving forward.

Tearing into Mr. Smith and trash-talking the insurance companies would have felt really good. The bottom line, however, was that I had made promises to the people I hired. The problem was mine.

> The energy you waste holding a grudge or getting revenge affects only your success, no one else's.

Watching my agents struggle financially felt just like standing on my neighbor's porch apologizing while my dad watched from the road. I had failed to follow through with my end of the bargain. Finding a way to help me keep my word changed everything. I had called every one of my agents before Dave made it back to Dallas.

Those who had already taken other jobs didn't come back, and I wished them well in their new careers. The other five followed me to the new company, and we had the beginnings of a strong team. I hadn't figured out exactly what it was we were doing yet, but I knew we had a great opportunity on our hands.

Scott, one of the guys I'd met working with Mr. Smith, called when he noticed my name missing from the weekly standings.

"You forget how to sell?" he asked.

"Nah. I found another company to work with."

"Seriously? You were killing it, man."

"Not making any money." I had a pretty good idea he wasn't, either. "Then Mr. Smith got all our commissions coming straight to him, and me and my guys were starving over here, so we had to make a change. You better look out for the same thing."

When I told him about the move, he asked what Colonial Life did.

"You know, sell insurance," I answered.

"Yeah, but what kind?"

> Failing your way forward is more important than sitting around waiting for the perfect plan to come together.

I shrugged like he could see me through the phone. "I don't know, man. You know, life insurance and disability and stuff. We sell it to businesses. Like their employee benefits."

Scott was quiet for a couple of seconds, then said, "That

sounds pretty good. What kind of contract you got?"

I tried to explain the district general agent's agreement I'd signed, but finally gave him Dave Moskowitz's number. Scott said Andy, Smith's other agency owner, would probably be interested too, so I told him I'd ask Dave to be on the lookout for their calls.

* * * * * * *

Both of them decided to make the move, but neither wanted the added expense and responsibilities I had taken on. Instead, they wanted to be a part of my district. Dave knew I would need plenty of help, so he suggested making them assistant managers. I might have been young and dumb with plenty to learn, but no way was I turning down that offer!

Scott and Andy had a lot of energy and were hungry, so they were a good fit for our team. We didn't pass Go and collect two hundred dollars or even look both ways before we crossed the street. We just charged blindly ahead. At first, in our ignorance, we made way more mistakes than we did sales. We learned from our missteps, though, and before long we were failing our way forward.

More sales meant we all had a chance to take an active part in helping our clients. That led to more sales, which led to helping more people. Our team became passionate about what we did. That seed the Browns had planted more than a year earlier began to grow.

At first, I didn't want to add new agents. We were a tight-knit group, and helping the team members we had didn't take too much time away from making my own sales. Even with money once again coming in, I was still behind financially, and I thought new agents would just slow me down.

Once again, Dave Moskowitz knew more about leadership than I did, and he gradually changed my thinking.

* * * * * * *

Over the next eighteen months, our district's sales exploded and we made a name for ourselves throughout the company. As a team, we talked as much about the people we helped as we did the sales we made. I couldn't believe how lucky I was to be working with the type of people who surrounded me. One thing I'm most proud of is that many of those people are now successful leaders throughout the Dallas area and around the country.

At some point, I realized I wasn't really working anymore. The passion I'd developed watching my agents find purpose and success transformed what I was doing into fun.

Except for the meetings. There is absolutely nothing fun about sitting still and being quiet long enough to have a good meeting. They are part of management, however, so I learned to bite the bullet and deal with them. Early on, I learned that catching up with agents, home office staff, and other managers is what makes spending all day in a windowless room bearable. That and getting the newest and most up-to-date information, of course. Much of that information comes from talking with everyone during breaks.

Something I picked up from the other field managers at one of my first territory meetings in Dallas taught me more than any ten management courses I'd taken. In fact, without the insight I received that day, I probably wouldn't have written this book.

HEATH'S TAKEAWAYS FOR SUCCESS

On Life "Being Fair"

Life isn't fair. For anybody. Ever.

Most of the time, those people who look like life has smiled bigger on them than on others are the ones who understand this concept. They decided that they would determine their own happiness and success. Not life. Not others. *Them*.

We all have tough days, and we all get down. That's the best time to remember that life not being fair is a *good* thing—maybe the best thing. If life *was* fair, most of us would have been done before we ever got started. But, since life *isn't* fair, we get a second chance. And a third one, and a fourth, and a fifth . . .

It's important to make sure you surround yourself with people who take every opportunity life gives them to succeed. If someone around you doesn't live that way, you need to move away from them, even if it hurts.

What three things are you most grateful for right now?

_____

_____

_____

What trait(s) do you have that is (are) special?

_____

_____

_____

If you're not happy with where you are in life, are you willing to stop your pity party and change your situation? Write more than yes or no here. List some of the ways you can begin to change.

_____

_____

_____

What habits do you have, or are you forming, that build you up?

_____

_____

_____

What habits do you have, or are you forming, that *don't* build you up?

_____

_____

_____

What steps do you need to take to change those poor habits, or to reinforce the good ones?

SIXTEEN

A FAMOUS QUOTE FROM ZIG— AND A REAL TEST FOR ME

It's been said that perception is reality. We all see the world through the lenses of our past experiences and current situations. When things are great, we assume everybody is doing well. If nothing else, we think, no one should feel hopeless when so much good is happening in the world. On the other hand, most of us can't understand folks who don't share our sense of imminent doom when the going gets tough.

Empathy is what lets us put aside our own emotions and expectations and identify with someone else's perception of the world. Nobody

> "You can't connect the dots looking forward. You can only connect them looking backward. So you have to trust that the dots will somehow connect in your future."[2]
>
> –Steve Jobs

is born with a well-developed sense of empathy. It's something we learn through experience as we move through life. Some people never get it. For a leader, it's an absolute necessity.

Looking through the prism of my team's success, I assumed we were just like any other district in any other area. Listening to the other field managers vent their frustrations, I began to understand how narrow my perception was. The complaints I heard about other organizations made two things clear.

First, there was no mistaking how professional my folks were. While other managers dealt with petty problems and disputes, I was able to focus on leading my team. Our results made the difference easy to see.

The other thing I figured out was that if I invested my energy in people instead of outcomes, like Dave Moskowitz did, our results would take care of themselves. Since there was no way my good luck attracting the right people would last, I wanted to learn everything I could about taking care of the people we had. For the first time, I realized that education is important. Whether it comes from formal schooling and a diploma or it's the result of consistent, concentrated study and reading, learning is the key. Those two books I'd found in my first real office were still on my shelf, and their titles made me think they would be a good place to start.

Someone once said, "The person who won't read good books has no advantage over one who can't read." Mark Twain usually gets the credit for those words, but nobody is really sure where they came from. I've never cared. I just knew back then that I needed all the advantages I could get, even if it meant reading every single day. I also knew the only way I could get where I wanted to go in life was by reading books about and by people who had already made the journey.

One thing Zig Ziglar wrote in *See You at the Top* caught my attention back then, and it seemed like a good way to take care of my team. The quote, which is included at the end of every email I send, is:

> *"You can have anything in life you want, if you will just help enough other people get what they want.*[3]

My attitude changed as soon as I started working to make this thought a habit. Nothing obvious happened at first while I was testing out my new belief. But this simple idea worked its way into my subconscious, weaving itself into the lessons I'd learned from my parents.

Leading such a strong team made it easy to integrate Zig's words into my thinking. It's not hard to help a bunch of motivated professionals with well-defined goals get what they want in life.

In fact, it took almost two years for this new commitment to be tested—really tested—for the first time.

I was in a meeting with members of our corporate training department. Since our district had more new agents achieving their goals than any other in the company, they asked me for input on a new training curriculum. When the vice president in charge of the project told me about a position being created to oversee the new system's development and implementation, a light popped on in my head.

"You've got to get Scott Wintory in here," I said.

The VP shook her head and looked at me like I was a nutcase. "You want to send Scott to corporate?"

She had a point. Scott was one of the guys who had been with Smith, and now he was one of my assistant managers.

He's still one of the best trainers I've ever worked with. His success rate with new agents was a big reason I'd been asked to help with the new training course. Losing him would be hard to overcome. But . . .

"Yep." I nodded. "He's too good to be stuck where he is. He's the absolute best person for this job."

She studied me for a couple of seconds, making sure I was serious. Then she replied, "Take some time to think this through. If you still think it's a good idea, tell him to send me a resume."

The reality of what I'd just done didn't sink in until I got home.

HEATH'S TAKEAWAYS FOR SUCCESS

On Zig Ziglar's Famous Quote

"You can have everything in life you want, if you will just help enough other people get what they want."

I've discussed this sentence, and Ziglar has published entire volumes on it, all of which are available online, at your local bookstore, or at your public library. I'll just say that adopting this statement as my life's philosophy changed my life and let me help hundreds of people change theirs. I'm not sure I can add much to that!

Is your focus on yourself or others?

_____

_____

_____

_____

What can you do daily to help more people get what they want from life?

_____
_____
_____
_____
_____
_____
_____
_____
_____
_____
_____
_____
_____
_____

What do you think the result will be?

_____
_____
_____
_____
_____
_____
_____
_____

SEVENTEEN

SOMETHING TO LOSE

Putting the Ziglar quote into practice for Scott just kind of happened. It seemed like the right thing to do.

Until I really thought about it, anyway. Common sense told me I was making a huge mistake.

It would be a lie to say I didn't struggle with the idea of talking Scott out of taking the job—even though I'd been the one who suggested him for the position to begin with! Getting Scott to say no would have been a win-win for me. I would look good for putting his name in the hat, but still keep the company's top assistant manager in my district. As tempting as that was, it went against everything I believe.

In September Scott moved to Columbia, South Carolina to oversee the creation and implementation of the new training system. That left me trying to fill the huge hole he'd left behind. I sweated bullets over how we could finish strong and win the Small Office of the Year award without our top assistant manager. I came to realize that worrying is a colossal waste of time.

Scott had given his team everything they needed to succeed. He had trained them so well that I was able to promote three different agents to take his place. Every one of them performed like veterans right from the start. That fourth quarter was the biggest quarter our team ever had, and we earned that Small Office of the Year award. It seemed too good to be true, except it wasn't.

The episode had a huge impact on me. No one would have questioned my wanting to keep Scott in my district. On the surface, talking him out of taking the job, or at least not giving him all the information and encouragement he needed, looked like the smart move. Smart, however, doesn't always mean right. That would have been kind of like taking my neighbor's money and leaving half his grass uncut.

> Putting others before yourself won't always work out like you want it to, but it will always work out better than holding someone back.

There was no guarantee things would work out like they did; there never is. I knew the next time might have a very different result, and that was OK. Instead of just a habit I tried to practice in the professional world, I embraced Zig's famous quote as my life's philosophy.

Something else had changed as well. Success had taken on a whole new meaning for me. It finally sunk in that success didn't mean having "mailbox money" or a huge bank account. All the indicators society teaches us to look for—nice cars, big houses, expensive vacations, designer clothes—are really just by-products of true success.

A lot has been written about my generation and how we don't see things quite like the ones that came before us. We tend to view businesses and money occupying different roles than our parents and grandparents saw. Technology has made our world smaller than theirs and changed how we see our place in society.

One thing hasn't changed since civilization first came into existence, however: the things we most want from life will come if we concentrate on helping other people get the same things for themselves.

With all these new insights and perspectives on life I figured, once again, that I had made it. I was making a difference in people's lives. I loved my job. I enjoyed the people I worked with. Only one thing really worried me. You might be thinking that sounds crazy. Only one thing to worry about? That sounds pretty good. But that single concern was big enough to cast a shadow over everything else.

At first, it was exciting to constantly attract the kind of people who made up our team. I don't care who you are, that much good luck makes you feel pretty special. The thing is, good luck never lasts, and I worried what would happen when mine ran out. For the first time in my life, I felt like I had something to lose, and it scared me.

Despite my fear, I determined to keep living my dream. Except for the looming specter of bad luck, I didn't see how life could get any better.

I got a hint in September 2009 at a meeting in Columbia, South Carolina.

EIGHTEEN

JUST WHEN THINGS GET COMFORTABLE...

Who did you eat lunch with yesterday? A good friend? A family member? A spouse or significant other? Was it a stranger? A group of people you don't really know? A group of friends? Who did you share your last plane, train, bus, or taxi ride with? What did they do? What was their passion? What did you have to offer them? What did they have to offer you?

Most of us put up a wall when we're thrown together with people we don't know. Technology demands our attention and keeps us moving at breakneck speed, so it's easy to get too caught up in our own lives to see what's going on around us. Too often, that means we not only miss an opportunity to help someone out, we deny them the opportunity to help us.

During dinner one night at a corporate meeting, a terri-

tory sales manager—a bit older, a bit more experienced—
told me he thought I'd do a great job in his role. I was grateful he had put that much thought into my abilities and was
willing to share, but I thought he was nuts. Most TSMs
were—and still are—in their late forties or older. I had just
turned twenty-three.

Bob went on to tell me about the position and what he
did on a daily basis. He also told me what he believed had
made him successful. He said the Southeast Region vice
president was making some changes and suggested I give
her a call. The next thing I knew, I had an interview for the
territory sales manager position in North Florida! That was
pretty heady stuff.

It doesn't matter if you're old or young, struggling or
successful, it always feels good when your hard work is
acknowledged by those further up the food chain. I didn't
really expect to get the job, but I couldn't know for sure
without taking my shot. Besides, nothing in my career to
that point had gone like I expected.

As I looked ahead and the initial excitement faded, a
couple of things came to me. First, I'm an East Texas boy.
That's what I am and what I had sworn I always would be.
Everything I wanted in life could be accomplished right
there at home. Nothing in Florida figured into my plans.

Second, a territory sales manager is a Home Office employee—a corporate man or woman. As an agent and a field
manager, I'd been self-employed. Between the car dealership and my experience with Mr. Smith, I'd vowed to myself
I would never work for someone else again.

On top of all that, I'd positioned myself to create one of
the biggest, most productive districts in the entire country over the next couple of years. That meant by the time
I turned thirty I would have accomplished all the financial

goals I'd set when making lots of money was still my definition of success. And after three years of stumbling around
and failing my way forward, I felt like I had a grip on things.

Finally, I was afraid of setting myself up for disappointment. The Southeast Region's vice president, Elana
D'Arciprete, was a tough, no-nonsense hardside. It was almost impossible to believe she would seriously consider
someone as young as me, especially since I had only been
with the company for less than two years.

Looking at all those factors, a big promotion became
a lot less exciting. In fact, taking a new position in a new
place with new people and less income potential didn't look
like a good move at all. I thought about canceling, but the
interview was already scheduled, and backing out would
send the wrong message to all the right people. Besides, I
still don't say no to something until I know what it is I'm
saying no to.

I called Elana to explain some of my thoughts. Sticking
to the money issue seemed like a good idea since my other
concerns might have given her ammunition against me. As
it turned out, she had her own reservations.

We got the pleasantries out of the way, and I dived in.
"So, how much money can I expect to make?" I asked.

Always direct, Elana said, "Now, how would you answer
that, Heath? You can expect to make as much as you work
for."

"I'm working my butt off right now," I said, "and I'm
pretty sure I'll be hitting some big paychecks coming up."

"You've done some remarkable things. Especially to be
so young."

And there it was. She let her words hang between us.

"I'm just getting started," I assured her.

"You know, it's a good thing you called."

Oh boy, I thought. *Here we go. She's going to tell me I'm too young.*

She drew in a deep breath and continued. "How do you feel about leaving your family? I mean, aren't they all in Texas?"

"In Troup," I said.

"So, do you think being so far away from them is going to bother you?"

Of course it would bother me.

But what I said was, "I'll miss them, if that's what you mean."

"I just wonder if the distance could be a problem."

I told her it wouldn't be, then asked the question I really wanted her to answer. "If you offer me the job, and I don't think it's a good idea right now, will that cause a problem?"

Elana laughed. "Not at all. That just means you're thinking about what's best more than you are about moving up the ladder. Now, I've got a question for you."

Uh oh. I almost felt like she had already started the interview.

"If I offer it to somebody else, are you going to go find the same job at another company?"

"No way!" I told her. "I'm not even sure it's the right place for me, so no worries there."

I think we both felt a lot better after that conversation. Knowing what my options were helped me prepare mentally for my trip to Jacksonville, Florida.

I should have been nervous, but I was too busy training my new managers and helping my folks meet all their goals for the year. On top of that, we had to be ready to get 2011 off to a big start. All of a sudden, it seemed, it was time for the interview.

It all seemed simple enough. Someone would meet me

at the airport and drive me to the North Florida Territory office. I planned to stay overnight and check things out (on the off chance I would wind up living there), then go home the next day and get back to work. Everything went exactly according to plan—until I got to the airport in Dallas.

My biggest fear about the interview process became reality before I even boarded the plane.

NINETEEN

THE BEST-LAID PLANS

Having plans fall apart when the schedule is tight can drive the most patient person crazy. Planning ahead keeps a lot of problems from happening, but some just can't be avoided. Even if I had mastered that important skill at twenty-three—which I hadn't—my day wouldn't have been any easier.

My phone rang as I boarded the plane in Dallas. Seeing Elana's name on the screen sent my heart into overdrive. I took a deep breath and hit the green button.

"Hello?"

"Hey, Heath. Got a change of plans."

I tried to ask what had happened, but she didn't give me a chance.

"The guy I had meeting you can't make it, so go ahead and rent a car when you land and bring me the receipt."

"OK," I said. "Is there a particular rental company you want me to use?"

"No, just grab something and come on."

"Got it."

Elana ended the call before I could ask any other questions. No worries. I could get more exploring done with my own ride.

I didn't see the fatal flaw in Elana's plan until I got to Jacksonville and the rental clerk told me I had to be twenty-five to rent a car. I was only twenty-three! Since my age had been my biggest fear about pursuing the new job, there was no way I could call Elana back and tell her what was going on. I was furious.

Fortunately, making quick decisions and coming up with alternate plans is a skill (often a liability) I have always had. Taxis are easy to find at an airport. Problem solved! But my solution created an unexpected consequence.

Jacksonville, Florida is, geographically, the largest city in the United States. It covers nearly eight hundred seventy-five square miles. Jacksonville International Airport is located at the city's northernmost point. The North Florida Territory office was located right on its southern border, forty-eight miles away.

I didn't think about the fare as we made our way through the city. The traffic, buildings, and people held my attention. That changed when we pulled up to the territory office and the cab driver said I owed him one hundred eight dollars! I thought the guy was kidding. And, I realized, I would have to take a cab back to the airport the next day. Even worse, I couldn't turn the receipt in for reimbursement without explaining to Elana why I hadn't rented a car like she told me to.

Just to be sure I wasn't getting ripped off or punked, I

looked over the seat at the meter and saw that, sure enough, the driver had given me the correct fare. It was tempting to try to argue the price down, but dealing with the car rental company and looking for a cab had put me behind schedule, and walking into the interview late wasn't an option. I gave the driver a credit card and got my thoughts together while he processed the payment.

Despite all the setbacks, I had my game face on by the time I walked into the office. I didn't plan to take the job, but I was going to make sure they offered it to me.

Elana had invited the territory recruiter and regional instructor to the interviews since their jobs required them to work closely with the new territory sales manager. Once everyone was introduced, she got down to business. Some of the questions were tough, but I was prepared.

One thing Dave Moskowitz taught me was to think and act like the person one level above me. It was good advice, and one of the reasons I'd been able to build a team so quickly. During the interview, I tried to stress the fact that I was already operating my district like a small territory, so I was ahead of the learning curve.

> One thing Dave Moskowitz taught me was to think and act like the person one level above me. It was good advice, and one of the reasons I was able to build a team so quickly.

I left the territory office feeling good about my chances.

I got the feeling from the recruiter and trainer that nobody believed the territory could be successful. That piqued my interest, but I still wasn't sure about becoming their next TSM. The regional instructor took me to dinner that night since I didn't have a car. It didn't take long to understand the North Florida group had a culture completely different than the one I was used to, especially when she asked if I needed her to pay for my meal with her company credit card.

In Texas, I always treated the regional instructor when we ate together. He worked hard helping train my new agents and, as a field manager, I made a lot more money than he did. It was hard for me to believe that the field managers in the North Florida Territory were all struggling so much that the RI had to pay for their meals. Seeing that the territory staff not only accepted this situation but took it for granted upset me.

What we expect is generally what we get out of life, and this group expected failure. My team members in Dallas went to work every day with the assumption they would achieve their goals, and most of them did. In North Florida, a lot of people watched their dreams drift away as they met their expectations of failure. Based on their experiences so far, they didn't know to expect more. I did, and I had a pretty good idea what effective leadership could do for these folks. While I appreciated the regional instructor's offer, I paid for my own meal, and then went back to my hotel to think about what I had learned.

One more thing I never could have planned for seemed like the perfect ending for a long day.

TWENTY

MANY THOUGHTS, LITTLE SLEEP

Two years earlier, I would have slept well that night. Instead, I laid awake thinking about everything that had happened over the last twenty-four hours. The promotion to TSM shouldn't have rated a second thought. Taking the job would mean breaking every promise I'd made to myself about moving forward in life. It would also require me to trade a growing income for an uncertain future.

The younger me—the one who saw money as the primary measure of success—would have run all the way back to Texas. Too much had changed for that to happen, though. As the conversation I'd had with the regional instructor ran through my head, the possibilities this territory offered sharpened into focus.

Lack of leadership meant quitting was an option for this group. Nobody held them accountable when it came to keeping their commitments to themselves, their clients, and their teammates. That didn't mean the North Florida team wasn't working hard or that nobody wanted to be great. It meant no one had shown them how or helped them believe they could.

I passionately believe in what our company does because I know, beyond any doubt, that somebody's life will improve when we do our jobs. A lot of people who work in our industry see the job as sales. That is, for sure, how agents and managers get paid, but I've always considered our primary function to be education. When we give the right people the right information in the right way, they will make the right decision. If we don't make that information available, we can't help them when they need us.

A big part of North Florida's population was going without the benefits we could offer them. That wasn't the case in Dallas. As a team, my district approached our work like I did: help people first and the rest will fall into place. That's not to say we weren't competitive or we didn't take a lot of pride in our accomplishments. We did, but we could have made a good living selling just about anything. We chose to work in the employee benefits side of the insurance industry because of the impact we had on people's lives.

Leaving the comfort of a district that had bought into my philosophy scared me to

> Feeling like a fraud after you make the choice to improve yourself is OK. Most successful people I know have gone through the same thing. We try to be the person we want to become, and sometimes we fall short. That doesn't make anyone a fraud. It just means we learn from our mistakes and work harder to reach the goal.

death. Moving away seemed like a betrayal . . . until I remembered the three new managers who did great things
when Scott moved to the Home Office. My team would do
just fine without me.

What, I had to wonder, could the North Florida Territory
do with a little passion and some leadership? It was exciting to think about. Taking the new job, if Elana made the
offer, would be a huge opportunity to help a lot of people
I wouldn't otherwise meet. I could expand my mission beyond what I had ever dreamed.

All the reasons I'd considered so far had been positive,
but the negative was there too, lurking below the surface.
What would happen when my good luck finally turned
sour? That thought ate away at my confidence, made me
stress when I should have been relaxing, and caused me
to question everything I had accomplished. It made me
ashamed, feeling like a fraud. It made me wonder if the best
thing would be to stay where I was and keep my head down.

That fear was a constant in my life. It rode around on my
back like a pet monkey, constantly looking over my shoulder. Now, I realize it was my good-luck-monkey. Back then,
I just knew I had to get rid of it. Surely, I thought, a new job
in a new place would be enough to change my luck. I mean,
everything crashing down around me was a scary enough
thought, but waiting for the disaster was even worse. If it
would just go ahead and happen, I could put it behind me
and start rebuilding.

I drifted off to sleep just before dawn, trying to figure out
how I'd talked myself into a job I thought I didn't want.

TWENTY-ONE

COMMUNICATION IS EVERYTHING

One of the things people love about working from home is spending the day in a T-shirt and jeans, or even pajamas! It sounds good, but self-perception directly affects our interaction with other people, even on the phone or through emails. Someone who is put together and professional will come across exactly the way they feel. So will a person who is laid back and sloppy. That's why I've always liked the saying, "Get up, dress up, show up, and never give up."

Before I made the call to Elana, I got dressed like I was going to another interview. When she answered, I told her I wanted the job. Not because it was a big promotion. I was ready to roll

> "If you look good, you feel good. If you feel good, you play good. If you play good, they pay good."[4]
> —Deion Sanders

my sleeves up and get to work.

Full disclosure here: I was kind of hoping she would say, "Great! When do you want to start?" Even back then I knew that's not how things work, but my fingers were crossed. Instead, she told me both candidates had done well and she would let me know when she'd made a decision. I hoped it wouldn't take long.

The hotel's concierge called a taxi for me, and I made the trek back across Jacksonville to the airport. The cab fare for those two days was more than two hundred dollars. It wasn't a lot of money, but the amount surprised me. Nobody calls a cab in East Texas. A friend, family member, or even a complete stranger will always give you a lift if you need it. Jacksonville, Florida was a long way from home.

Back in Dallas, I dug in, making sure the district finished the year strong. We were so busy I didn't have time to worry about North Florida. About a month after the interview, Elana called. She told me she wanted to fly into Dallas-Fort Worth International Airport, have lunch and talk, and then head back home. I'd never had a spur-of-the-moment, on-the-fly meeting like that, so I didn't know what to expect.

All I knew, as I headed to the airport, was that I was more than one hundred and fifty miles from the restaurant where we were supposed to meet, and there would be about a million cars on I-20. I hurried into the traffic.

My nerves got tight as I drove through Dallas. I still felt like I'd done really well in the interview, but Elana's tone of voice that morning indicated something different. I expected her to tell me the job had gone to the other guy.

From her perspective, that was probably the safest call. He was a good ten years older than me, and he'd been with the company longer. My ego would be dented, but I was in a good place with nothing to worry about. Other than that good-luck-monkey, who always seemed to be lurking about.

Traffic is terrible in Dallas on a good day, and this day was a bad one. I slid into the restaurant late, trying to talk myself down before road rage consumed me. Running behind made the tension even worse. Fortunately, Elana understood life in the metroplex and how little warning she'd given me.

After we ordered, she congratulated me on the district's numbers and asked where I thought we'd finish. I told her we weren't settling for anything less than number one. She frowned when I said how lucky I was to have such a good team, but seemed to like that we were determined to take the top spot. Then her expression turned serious and she leaned back, studying me.

Finally, she asked, "How do you think your interview went?"

I tried not to flinch as I said, "I thought it was pretty good."

She nodded. "Most of it was. But you said something that really bothered me, and I wanted to talk to you about it."

My mind raced, trying to figure out where I'd screwed up. I shouldn't have worried; Elana didn't make me wait.

"You've done really well in a short time," she said. "But that doesn't mean you know everything you need to know. You can't ever stop learning." She sipped her water. "If I went back in the field today, I'd still pick up something from every new agent I trained."

"OK." I didn't have a clue what this woman was talking about, but I knew enough to wait and hear her out.

"When I asked you why you were the best candidate for the job, you said you already knew all about being a territory sales manager. And I've got to tell you, that's a bunch of crap."

Huh?

I shook my head. "When did I say . . . "

And then it hit me. She'd misunderstood what I had been trying to say about running my *district like it was a territory.* I was about to correct her when something else crashed into me just like a sledgehammer to the head.

She hadn't misunderstood. *I* had failed to communicate clearly.

At that point, I knew I wouldn't get the job, but I still wanted to explain what I'd meant. I'll always be grateful that Elana was willing to listen. When I finished, she had several questions, and I made sure my answers conveyed exactly what I meant. Her whole demeanor changed when she understood what I'd been trying to say. We talked a little more, and then it was time for Elana to head back to the airport.

> I was about to correct her when something else crashed into me, and it hit just like a sledgehammer to the head. *She* hadn't misunderstood. *I* had failed to communicate clearly.

I had arrived expecting to be told I would remain a field manager in Dallas. It was a relief when Elana said she was still sorting things out and would be in touch. I wasn't hopeful as I made my way back to East Texas, but technically, I was still in the running.

* * * * * * *

I had always taken for granted that clear, effective communication is important, especially in sales. It was painful to learn how little I really understood what that meant. My reaction had been to correct the mistake as quickly and forcefully as possible. Once I went into damage control, I'm pretty sure I looked and sounded like I could conquer the world. But all that swagger was gone when I got back to the car. That good-luck-monkey of mine called shotgun, and it wouldn't shut up.

Elana might have gotten the message that she had seen things wrong and I was just conveying that I had what a TSM needed to succeed, but deep down, I knew it was really me who had it all wrong. A territory sales manager is responsible for hundreds of agents and tens of thousands of clients. To be effective, his or her leadership must be built on knowledge and skill. Mine, I believed, had been built on luck.

Over and over I kept telling myself that all the bravado and cockiness, along with my belief that I could make a difference in the world, was a fraud. Just like me. When my luck finally ran out, everybody would know the truth.

It took some work, but I finally got my head right. Before I made it back to the office, I managed to put a gag in that negative inner-passenger of mine and convince myself that I just needed to ride the wave until it crested and then deal with whatever fallout would come later.

As the days went by, I questioned my decision to go all-in for the promotion. Abandoning what I'd worked so hard to build might have been the worst idea I'd ever had. No matter how much I rationalized, however, I couldn't get away from Zig Ziglar's quote. It tied in perfectly with the lessons I'd learned from my parents, lessons I had made my own. If I really claimed those words as my life's mission, it was time to put up or shut up.

In truth, turning my back on the opportunity to help

even more people would confirm my fear that I was a fraud—and that was something I couldn't accept.

If by some wild chance the job was offered, I was ready to go.

TWENTY-TWO

LOOKING THAT MONKEY IN THE EYE

No one lives completely free of fears and doubts. But good leaders know how to push those things aside and move their people forward no matter what else might be happening. Allowing a team to worry about a potential management change is one of the best ways to tear it apart.

Everyone still has the same job. Their goals stay the same. Income needs don't change. But tell them the leader, even several levels up, is leaving, and things have a way of shutting down.

That's why I'd kept quiet about the possibility of moving. It was tough, but it was best. Elana agreed, so getting a phone call at my office about a week after that lunch meeting in the airport restaurant shocked me.

Whatever it was, I assumed Elana would call to tell me her decision. Instead, someone from Human Resources was on the phone telling me what my salary and benefits would be when I moved to Jacksonville. I didn't know what to say. I thought I must have missed a call, or maybe a message, or at least an email. My biggest, most immediate concern was making sure nobody in the office picked up on the conversation.

Finally, I got myself together enough to say I needed some time to think it over. The HR rep said that was fine. I had forty-eight hours. The rest of the day passed in a blur. Everything made sense when the offer was hypothetical. Once it became real, I needed to get my head around it all over again.

My parents encouraged the move. Dad told me to take any chance I had to travel. He and Mom hadn't had that opportunity, and they didn't want me to miss out. Mom said it was fine with her as long as she could fly out whenever she wanted to visit. She loves the beach, so I'm pretty sure having a free place to stay influenced her enthusiasm just a little bit.

My roommate, Ty, had been my best friend since middle school. Without his help, I never would have graduated.

Sitting in the living room after work that night, I kept it simple. "Got a call from HR today."

"And?" Ty didn't take his eyes from the television.

"Well, I guess I got the job. She told me all about how much they'll pay me and how they'll take care of moving everything."

"So?" Ty took a swallow of his drink and looked over in my direction. "You going to take it?"

In addition to being my best friend and one of my assistant managers, Ty had leased a house with me about two months earlier. Whatever decision I made would affect him in a lot of ways.

I thought about it for a couple of seconds and then blurted out, "I'll go if you will."

It made perfect sense. I needed good field managers on the ground as quickly as I could get them. Ty would be promoted and have a huge opportunity to grow. Instead of going into all that, he just nodded. "OK."

I waited a couple of seconds to make sure he was serious. Then I lifted my glass in his direction. "We're going to Jacksonville!"

The next morning, I called HR and accepted the job. They gave instructions on setting up the move and finding a place to live in North Florida. My next call was to Elana. We agreed I would start at the first of the year, just a couple of weeks away. With Christmas so close and the district running at full speed, I had a lot to do and not much time to get it all done.

* * * * * * *

Telling the folks in my district was hard. Yes, I knew not to worry, but they were the faces of my first real success, and they were good friends. They took the news well, and most were happy for both Ty and me. It was a tough day, but I kept reminding myself of my mission—to help as many people as I could. Also, in the back of my mind, I knew I was ready to look that good-luck-monkey in the eye and see which of us was tougher.

Ty and I rolled into Jacksonville with a truckload of stuff the night before New Year's Eve in 2010. The executive apartment we'd be staying in wouldn't be ready until the next morning, so we checked into a hotel and then went to find supper. I don't remember what we ate that night, but I do remember we were pretty quiet.

It had been an exhausting day, and I'm pretty sure both of us were thinking about what we'd just done. Ty served two tours in Iraq as a United States Marine, but Fort Worth was about the farthest I'd ever been from home until my interview with Elana.

I felt like I'd moved to the other side of the world.

HEATH'S TAKEAWAYS FOR SUCCESS

On Dreams

Ellen Johnson Sirleaf, President of Monrovia and the first female to serve as an elected head of state on the African continent, said, "If your dreams don't scare you, they aren't big enough."

Being a native Texan, big is all I know. Still, sometimes I catch myself trying to avoid failure and disappointment by keeping my dreams a little too realistic. I love President Sirleaf's quote because it reminds me what is important.

It's OK if you don't know how you're going to get what you want. It's even OK if you're not exactly sure what that is. Your dreams should grow with you, so they're going to change anyway. It's more important to dream bigger than you think you can achieve. I want you to come up with the craziest, biggest thing you can think of, and then make your dream bigger than that.

You don't achieve what you can't see, so building a dream board is essential. Instead of going out on New Year's Eve, my wife and I stay in and put together our dream boards for the coming year. We load them with pictures representing the things we want to achieve, the places we want to go, and the things we want to own. Then, we put our boards in a place we can see them every day. Neither of us can forget what we want for the next year.

I also find ways to always talk about my biggest dreams. That sounds silly to some, but it keeps me focused on what I'm trying to achieve. Even better, it's been proven that the more you say something, the more you believe it. So, dream the biggest dream you can, make sure it stays in front of you every day, and put it out there by talking about it every chance you get.

What is the one thing you want most out of life?

_____

_____

_____

_____

Starting today, what steps will you take to achieve it? What steps have you already taken?

_____

_____

_____

_____

What do you find yourself dreaming about throughout the day? What steps will you take today to achieve those dreams? What steps have you already taken?

_____

_____

_____

_____

_____

_____

When you begin talking about your dreams, who will be there to encourage you?

_____

_____

_____

_____

Who will discourage you and tell you you're crazy?

_____

_____

_____

_____

Are you willing to distance yourself from those who won't support your dreams?

TWENTY-THREE

PULLING THE PUZZLE PIECES IN PLACE

The apartment Ty and I would be living in for the next three months was furnished, so we only brought the things we would need until we found something permanent. Since we were two single guys, I won't pretend we spent a lot of time or energy unpacking and putting things away the next day. By the time we got it all unloaded, took the trailer back to U-Haul, and went by the territory office to check things out, however, most of the day was gone.

My first New Year's Eve away from home was exciting, even if neither of us knew any good places to go. We didn't even know anybody we could ask! So, we figured it was time to go exploring.

We learned a lot about Jacksonville and gave 2011 a proper welcome, then hit the office the next morning ready to take on the world. Ty already knew his job. He just had to learn the area he would be working in.

The first thing I had to do was meet the territory staff and managers. Without their best effort, without their success, we wouldn't be able to change lives like the team in Dallas was doing.

The office administrator was a temp, but she had learned a lot about the workings of the territory in a short time. Her knowledge and great patience got me through those first few weeks while I tried to figure out which way was up. She quickly became a permanent employee and kept the office running until she went out into the field as an agent.

I had already met the territory recruiter and regional instructor during my interview. I expected a pretty easy conversation when I sat down with Meredith, the recruiter. Instead, she blindsided me before we even got started.

"I kind of hate to tell you this," she said, "but I had decided to go somewhere else before they told us the last territory sales manager was leaving."

That really bothered me because I liked Meredith and was looking forward to working with her.

"Please tell me you're kidding," I said.

"No. I hadn't even planned to sit in on your interview." She shrugged. "I just wondered what another TSM would be like."

"So what's got you wanting to work somewhere else?" I asked.

As we talked, I realized that many of her reasons for leaving were the same things that made me want to move to Jacksonville. She saw those same things as well when I shared some of the plans I had for the territory and what role she would play in building a winning team.

Before we ended that day, Meredith agreed to stay on board.

Almost immediately, we had a great working relationship, and I developed a huge amount of respect for her. Meredith's steady manner and integrity meant her reaction to a given situation became the standard I judged my actions against. She'll never know (thankfully!) how many times I avoided trouble by trying to imagine what she would say about something I wanted to do.

After meeting with my regional sales trainer, we both agreed that our philosophies and expectations weren't a good match, and a change needed to be made. The team in Texas had been successful because we all worked toward common goals, and I knew

> As a leader, especially a young leader, it's important to surround yourself with people who are already the person you're striving to become.

North Florida had to develop the same dynamic if we had any hope of turning things around. I had a good idea who could make that happen.

Nick was an agent I'd hired in Texas, and he was one of the best salespeople I'd ever met. On top of that, he was an incredible trainer. Finding someone who's really good in both areas is rare, and when you do, that person is an incredible resource. It only took a couple of phone calls to get Nick on his way to Jacksonville.

With the right regional instructor in place, our territory staff was as good as I'd ever seen. In addition to Ty, we also had two veteran field managers who formed the foundation we would build on. It was a great starting place, but that's all it was—a starting place. We had a lot of work ahead of us.

The North Florida Territory had not hit a single sales goal in three and a half years. My district (one of the units that comprise a territory) in Texas had never missed one.

In 2010, we generated more new accounts and more new agents than the entire *territory* I had just taken over! Those were some scary numbers—but they were also a great challenge.

I'm proud to say nobody who formed the nucleus of that team ever looked back.

TWENTY-FOUR

IGNORANCE ON FIRE AND KNOWLEDGE ON ICE

It's easy to get so caught up in achieving a goal that everything else fades away, including the consequences of success. At some point in life, we've all reached out and grabbed the gold ring only to look around, suddenly wondering what in the world to do with it. That's how I felt once I had time to sit in my new chair behind my new desk in my new office and just breathe for a second. I'll bet it's the same feeling known by every dog that's ever chased a car and actually managed to catch it.

The plans and dreams were all great, but the reality was that I had to learn some things about running a territory, and I had to learn them quickly. Unfortunately for my team, failing my way forward was still my preferred method of figuring things out. Elana put it best at my first regional managers meeting. I knew most of the other TSMs, but she had us all introduce ourselves.

When we were done, she pointed to me and another new manager and said to the others, "Now, y'all are going to have to handle your own business for the next few months. Over here I've got knowledge on ice and ignorance on fire. They're going to be taking up most of my time for a while." She stepped to my chair, put her hand on my shoulder, and said, "Especially this one."

> Letting the fear of making a mistake hold them back is the biggest mistake most people make. That's ego, and ego and success usually don't work well together. Lose the ego. Make mistakes—that's the quickest way to figure something out. Ignorance on fire will almost always trump knowledge on ice.

I wasn't sure whether she meant that as a compliment or a put-down, but I decided I'd rather be charging ahead and learning from my mistakes than hanging back, gathering information, and waiting for the "right time." Today, I claim the title of ignorance on fire—with pride. Our society puts so much stress on never making a mistake that people and businesses become paralyzed. Something I've always told my new managers and agents is that not making a mistake means they aren't working hard enough. Get out there and make something happen, even if it's wrong.

An organization's culture isn't an easy thing to change. It's a lot like a habit; once it's established, you do or think the same thing over and over every day. If a team has a winning culture, it can't be stopped. If team members accept excuses and failure—whether success is measured by achieving sales goals or helping people—winning is nearly impossible. Change your habits and you will watch your life change.

Both veteran field managers had been with the company longer than I had. One of them had even applied for the TSM position. I wasn't sure how anybody would respond to me or the changes I wanted to make. Regardless, the culture in the North Florida Territory was going to change. It happened sooner than anyone thought.

In the first quarter of 2011, the veterans stepped up and delivered like a bunch of pros. For the first time in more than three years, the territory not only met its sales goal, we exceeded it. We did the same in the second and third quarters, too.

Almost everyone has heard that success breeds success. In North Florida, we got to see that old maxim in action. It had been a long time since the people in our field force achieved their personal goals, and that led to success—by my definition, anyway—for most of our team members.

Those who wanted to advance got promoted. Agents and managers met their personal financial goals. Folks who wanted to help people or support a particular cause could contribute time, money, or both. As a team, we helped countless customers in North Florida deal with the financial burdens that come with serious illness or injury.

It was an exciting time. Once again, my good luck held out long enough for me to find and hire all the right people. But the longer it took for the streak to end, the more I dreaded what would eventually have to happen. That good-luck-monkey was getting heavy. I found myself hoping some kind of ill fortune would show up—just to knock the thing off my back.

I didn't know it then, but the two of us were about to run into a brick wall, something that would have nothing to do with luck.

TWENTY-FIVE

SO LONG, GOOD-LUCK-MONKEY

The territory sales manager position in Atlanta came open near the end of 2011, and Elana put a lot of work into finding the right candidate to fill the position. I knew my friend Scott, who had left Texas to work in the corporate training department, was ready to get back in the field. I also knew he would be a great TSM. I mentioned him to Elana a couple of times, but never really got a response.

As she was leaving my office one afternoon, I said, "Have you got anybody in mind for Atlanta yet?"

She shook her head.

"Well, I still think Scott would do a great job."

She nodded. "I'll look at everybody when I have time."

"I keep telling you," I said. "He'll be a lot better than me."

Before I go any further, I need to take a step back and fill in a hole or two. The first six months I was in Jacksonville,

Elana and I talked every day. She taught me a lot, and she listened while I talked my way through a lot of situations. Sometimes she watched me screw things up and let me learn a hard lesson. Sometimes she told me just how foolish—not usually her word—I would be to follow through with something that was about to get me in trouble.

Even though she didn't know how badly it scared me, Elana was the only person in the world who knew I gave luck all the credit for the good things that had happened to me. She had even scolded me for it several times, but I never truly heard what she was saying.

I couldn't miss it this time. Elana went very still and gave me a look that left no doubt she would rather strangle me than continue talking. Instead, she marched me back into my office and slammed the door behind her. I didn't know what was about to happen, but I knew it was going to be bad.

In a voice like thunder, she said, "Don't you ever—and I mean ever—let me hear you say anybody is better than you at your job. Not even your friend Scott."

She jabbed her finger at me and took a step closer.

I moved two steps back.

"You have a talent," she continued. "I know you think it's just good luck that keeps bringing good people in, but luck's got nothing to do with it. That's your gift, so don't let me ever hear you say anything about good luck again."

I drew a breath to argue with her, but taking another step back seemed like a better idea. Elana must have read my mind, because she explained why my argument would have been wrong.

"You get one great person because you're lucky. Maybe two if you're on a roll—but that's it. You don't surround yourself with a whole team of talent because you're on a hot streak. Hell, if that was the case, I'd have you buying my lottery tickets every week and picking horses at the track."

She was still pretty mad, but she didn't look like she wanted to kill me anymore, so I gave her sort of a half-grin. She didn't smile back.

Instead, she poked her finger at me again and launched into another tirade. "Luck always runs out. *Always*. You keep finding good people to work with because you recognize talent and passion when you see it, then you bust your butt to help the people develop it. That's what you're good at. All this running around saying 'I'm just lucky' is a bunch of crap, and I don't want to hear it anymore."

I wasn't sure if it was safe to speak yet, but I muttered, "OK."

"Did you hear me?" she barked. "I mean it, Heath. If I hear any more about this, I'm done with you. I swear." She raised her right hand just like she was in front of a bailiff swearing to tell the truth, the whole truth, and nothing but the truth. "I will never speak to you again."

"OK," I said more loudly. Once again, I decided saying as little as possible was the safest option.

Later, when things were quiet and I'd had time to digest her words, I pinched myself to make sure I wasn't dreaming. It seemed too good to be true. Everything wasn't going to come crashing down just because I'd used up all my good luck. I could build as big as I wanted, achieve as much as I wanted, help as many people as I wanted, and nothing bad was going to happen. No more nightmares of going back to East Texas with my tail tucked between my legs, starting all over again.

> Talent is worthless without hard work.

That moment, when I accepted who I am and embraced what I'm good at, I felt truly free for the first time in my life. The only limits I had to worry about were the ones I put on myself, and they didn't bother me. I could get rid of those just as easily as I'd created them. It was a defining moment when I finally understood that I'm the only one with the power to decide whether I achieve greatness or maintain the status quo.

I turned my head to ask my good-luck-monkey what he thought of that, and what he was going to do about it, but I couldn't find him. The little coward had run away.

I've never missed him. He was lousy company anyway.

HEATH'S TAKEAWAYS FOR SUCCESS

On Mentors

Mentors are crucial to finding success. I learn something from almost everyone I come in contact with, but the three mentors I talk about in *Ignorance on Fire*—Dave Moskowitz, Elana D'Arciprete, and Mike Keller—have been critical in helping me achieve success early in life. Between them, they have more than one hundred years of experience in business and management. That's a lot of knowledge for me to access!

So, how do you find a mentor? First, you have to look for one. Mentors don't just show up on your doorstep. You have to find somebody who has already achieved the goals you've set for yourself. Be careful, though! Don't assume that professional success means personal success. You need to be sure that your prospective mentor has the same beliefs and values you do both professionally and personally.

Occasionally, you might need to work with a mentor for a specific aspect of your life. That person's beliefs in other areas won't affect you as much. However, it's still important to be sure that person has always demonstrated strong ethics and integrity. If you have questions about someone, believing they lack in those areas, they aren't fit to be your mentor.

Do you have a mentor?

_____

_____

If so, in what area(s) of your life do they provide guidance?

_____

_____

_____

_____

In what other areas could they could help? Do you need another mentor to help achieve other goals?

_____

_____

_____

_____

If you don't have a mentor right now, who might be a good candidate?

_____

_____

_____

_____

What do you hope to learn from that person(s)?

_____

_____

_____

_____

How do you plan to approach that person?

_____

_____

_____

_____

Remember: you can't take the next step—learning from your mentor—until you take the first one!

TWENTY-SIX

SEE PROBLEM, FIX PROBLEM

Walking around under a cloud of dread is just about the worst thing in the world. Waiting for a bad performance review, a looming confrontation with a friend or coworker, results of a test, a big interview—these things can drain the energy and joy from even the strongest person. When that weight is lifted, though, it's almost like having wings.

For a few days after my conversation with Elana (I guess *her* conversation with me would be more accurate), I had more energy than normal and plenty of excitement. That feeling should have lasted a long time, but it didn't. I found myself dragging, dreading things that should have been fun, or at least easy to handle.

Meanwhile, the whole team, from the newest agent to the territory staff, was pumped, and it showed. Not only were we exceeding our goals in every metric, we were doing it because our team members made a habit of consistently doing the little, most basic things that lead to hitting goals. Luck wasn't any part of it. What was wrong with me?

Nothing really stuck out, so I decided I was probably just tired and needed to rest for a few days. Well, that wasn't happening in December, not when we were so close to finishing off an outstanding year. I had a suspicion we could finish in the top ten. That was pretty exciting for a territory that finished next to last the previous year. I figured some needed rest would be my Christmas present to myself.

* * * * * * *

Starting strong in a new year after a record-breaking performance can be a challenge, so I called Elana to get advice on how to not screw things up in January. Her answer was short and seemed a little bit silly at the time. Instead of telling me what I should be doing, she warned me against thinking I had everything figured out.

I wasn't worried about that. We'd already had the discussion about always learning and getting better. Anyway, I had the best North Florida team in the company's history, and they hummed along like the finest, most well-oiled machine ever assembled. Nothing to worry about there.

In truth, I didn't spend much time thinking about Elana's advice, even though I'd been concerned enough to ask for it. Other things demanded my attention.

As the year came to a close, my prediction for our great finish proved inaccurate. I had been too conservative. The North Florida Territory finished 2011 in fifth place in the company. (And no, the company didn't change the total number of territories to six!) We were all proud and ready to do even better in 2012.

I was still exhausted, though, and feeling overwhelmed.

The holidays were restful, and they gave me some time to spend reflecting on the territory team and my place in it. That's when I realized what was killing my energy. The ways I interacted with the people in my office dragged me down and kept any of us from moving forward the way we should. Changing things around to start the new year sounded like a terrible idea since we had accomplished so much so quickly, but something had to give. My blood pressure was way up, and I didn't want to deal with a serious health problem— or worse.

I came up with a plan that might allow us to make the changes we needed without disrupting our momentum. In early January I pulled my territory administrator, recruiter, and regional instructor in the conference room, closed the door, and had them all turn off their cell phones. I asked them to look around and write down the job description for each person in the room, including me.

> A feeling of having things all figured out means you're not pushing yourself enough. Letting it lull you into no longer learning and looking for ways to grow will always end badly.

When we were done, I asked everyone to write out his or her own job description.

The differences in what everybody came up with were amazing, and the problem was immediately obvious. Just about everything that should have been in their own descriptions was found, in some way—you guessed it—in mine. I had made the mistake of taking on everyone else's tasks.

I thought I was doing them all a favor. Instead, I kept them from growing and becoming experts in their fields.

In addition to costing my staff the professional respect of the people they were supposed to be helping, I was nearly working myself to death.

They understood what was happening, and we spent the rest of the day getting responsibilities properly aligned. With my workload lessened, I was able to concentrate on the things that would keep our team moving forward at a good pace. The changes brought instant improvements with none of the speed bumps I'd been worried about.

I'll admit, I was pretty pleased with myself for finding the problem and getting it fixed so quickly and easily. Running a territory had turned out to be pretty easy. It hadn't taken long at all for me to get it all figured out.

TWENTY-SEVEN

LESSONS LEARNED WHILE . . . PUMPING GAS?

In the movies, life-changing realizations and ideas come with heroic music against a sweeping backdrop, and then everything about the hero's life changes. In the real world, those moments just kind of happen—no warning, no fanfare, and no music, unless a radio is playing somewhere close by! Just regular people in regular places. Like at a gas pump, for instance.

Early in 2012, I went to Brunswick, Georgia to meet with one of my field managers. I'd agreed to help him pay for a contest if his team met certain criteria, and they hit those goals out of the park. Since the money wasn't figured into the territory budget, I paid him from my personal account.

When I stopped for gas on my way home that night, I used my corporate credit card. Company rules specifically prohibit using it for a personal vehicle, which I was in, but I figured it would be OK since I'd just helped pay for a company contest. Then I froze, fingers still gripping the nozzle's trigger. My mind went racing back.

One day when I was eight or nine, my dad took me to the gas station in Troup. I needed gas before I headed out to cut grass, and he was going to fill up his truck. He told me to toss my fuel can in the back and ride with him.

At the time, he was operations manager of a trucking firm. One of his perks was the use of a company pickup truck, and it wasn't only for work. He could use the truck just like it was his. What made the deal really sweet was he also got a company credit card to buy gas, even for personal use. He worked for a great company.

> Even when you're doing something as routine as pumping gas, you do the right thing because it's the right thing to do, not because someone might be watching.

When we got to the station, Dad swiped the company card and filled the truck. I had already gotten the top off my gas can, and when the pump clicked off I reached for the hose.

"Wait," Dad said as he put the nozzle back in its slot, turning off the pump.

"What are you doing?" I asked.

I was relieved when he took another card out of his wallet and swiped it through the reader. The only reason I'd tagged along was so he could buy my gas for the day! That was five bucks I could keep in my own pocket.

He held the nozzle out for me. "That's not a company lawnmower you're using."

"It's just five dollars."

Dad fixed me with a hard stare. "Doesn't matter if it's five cents. That card is only for filling up this truck. Your grass-cutting business isn't part of the deal."

I couldn't figure out how what he was saying made any sense. While the gas can filled, I looked around and asked, "But how would anybody know?"

At the time, there's no way Dad could have known how much his answer would change my life. He kept that stare fixed, and said, "They probably wouldn't, but you do the right thing because it's the right thing to do. It doesn't matter whether anybody else sees it or not."

So . . . back at the gas pump in Florida, I almost threw that nozzle to the ground when I realized what I was about to do. Yes, I had just spent my own money for a company expense, but nothing about that made it OK to break the rules. The consequences of actions the company considered fraudulent included termination.

Our accounting department handles millions of transactions each year, so the chance they would have taken the time to look into this particular purchase was just about nonexistent. But what mattered was doing the right thing.

The lesson Dad taught me that summer sounded crazy back then.

Thirteen years later, the man was a genius.

HEATH'S TAKEAWAYS FOR SUCCESS

On Character

We all know the difference between right and wrong, and every day we're given many opportunities to choose one or the other. Consistently making the right decision doesn't just happen. You have to know what you believe in and never stray from that foundation—*no matter what.* That's called character, and it starts with the smallest decisions we make on a daily basis.

Cutting a corner when nobody's looking, not putting 100 percent into the small tasks that won't get much attention, or even not counting all of your golf strokes . . . these things don't seem like a big deal. Our brain loves habits, though, and those little actions begin forming the habit of dishonesty. When bigger, more serious situations come up, most of us will react by doing what we've consistently done in the past. Those tiny decisions—the ones that didn't seem like much at the time—are what set us up to handle the big things.

Start preparing for the big decisions now, if you haven't already, by paying attention to the smallest choices you make every day, and using them to build good habits.

What are some of the choices you've made today or will face before the day is over?

_____

_____

_____

_____

_____

What were, and will be, character-building choices?

_____

_____

_____

What were, or might be, character-destroying choices?

_____

_____

_____

If you find you're making more easy choices than good ones, don't worry. Nobody makes the right call every time, and it's something you can work on. What are three things you've found in *Ignorance on Fire* you can use to help make good choices consistently?

_____

_____

_____

_____

_____

_____

Life moves pretty fast for most of us, and it's easy to re-act to situations without evaluating our choices as we make them. If you want help remembering to respond thoughtfully instead of reacting, put a rubber band around your wrist as you start your day. Switch it to the other wrist every time you do something that doesn't build good character traits. If you find yourself moving the rubber band frequently at first, it won't be long before you leave it mostly on one wrist. If you find you don't have to move it often, the rubber band will be a reminder to live each day thoughtfully and with purpose.

TWENTY-EIGHT

YOU CAN'T LEAD FROM BEHIND

Even when we're separated by time and distance, the people and events that define us are always close. We spend our lives making decisions based on lessons learned from the past. How we interpret those lessons and how we use them usually determines whether we make good choices or bad ones.

Dad was twelve hundred miles away when I remembered the conversation we had about doing the right thing, but it felt like he was standing right beside me, watching and waiting to see what I would do. I was an adult and an executive with a Fortune 500 company, but I put the nozzle back and canceled that sale in a hurry. I swiped my own card through the reader and started pumping gas.

Waiting on the tank to fill, I thought about what the wrong decision could have meant if the accounting department somehow tracked that transaction. It didn't take much imagination. The results of ignoring the guidelines couldn't have been made any plainer when I took the TSM position.

The realization of how close I came to jeopardizing my career hit me in the chest like a bolt of lightning. Losing everything, including my reputation, was about the worst thing I could imagine. The people who depended on me and had bought in to my philosophy would suffer as well. Strapping on my seatbelt, my arms broke out in goose bumps.

It's unbelievable how a small act can carry colossal consequences. Pumping that gas became a defining moment for me. Whatever good choices I'd made up to that point had been based on instinct, not deep-seated or well-thought-out principles. Moving forward, I knew a different, more solid perspective would guide my decisions.

> Leadership happens up front, not in the rear.

* * * * * * *

With the combination of these great new insights and the time to concentrate on my job instead of doing everyone else's, I expected to roll right through 2012. I had things well in hand and the North Florida Territory was going to the top.

Remember what I just said about actions having consequences?

Things never quite got off the ground in January, and February was over before I realized it had started. I didn't understand how much trouble we were in until early March. Our sales were nowhere near our quarterly goal. I had done exactly what Elana warned me against doing. While I was strutting around like a bantam rooster, secure in the knowledge that everything was under control, my territory was in the process of crashing and burning.

Panic was an appropriate response . . . for a few seconds. And then it was time to set things right. I met with each field manager and made sure they understood our situation. Since my success was based completely on theirs, I did everything possible to help them make the sales we needed. It was a crazy, exhausting few weeks.

> What I figured out was I would never have it all figured out. If I ever felt like I did, I would lead my team to failure. That was exactly what Elana had tried to tell me. Leadership happens up front, not in the rear.

All our work—made exponentially harder by my failure to follow Elana's advice—almost paid off. But not quite. We finished the quarter at 98 percent of our sales goal.

After four consecutive quarters of doing more than we needed, we dropped the ball because I didn't follow through with the same practices and expectations that had led to such a great year in 2011. It was the first goal I ever missed, and it stung. Badly. I vowed we would never miss another one, and I tried to learn everything I could from the experience.

What I figured out was I would never have it all figured out. If I ever felt like I did, I would lead my team to failure. That was exactly what Elana had tried to tell me. Leadership happens up front, not in the rear. Staying in front of the pack is impossible if the leader isn't constantly learning and moving forward.

* * * * * * *

I didn't think I could be any prouder of the North Florida team than the performance they delivered in 2011, but I was wrong. They dug in, and we exceeded our goals each of the next three quarters. We also blew out our yearly sales goal for 2012 and finished at number three in the company, two spots up from 2011 and thirty-eight spots higher than in 2010.

The team didn't miss another sales goal the rest of the time I was in Jacksonville.

I assumed that would be a long time, but things have a way of moving in odd and unexpected directions.

TWENTY-NINE

HOMEWARD BOUND

If failure was permanent, most of us would have thrown in the towel before finishing kindergarten. We only fail when we decide our mistakes are the final destination instead of just another part of the journey. Likewise, success is not the pot of gold at the end of the rainbow. It's found in the day-to-day habits we form traveling through life.

As 2012 drew to a close, our entire management team worked hard to make certain the mistake I made in the first quarter wasn't repeated. We had plans in place, and everyone made sure they hit the ground running on January 2.

Our work paid off; the transition was seamless. 2013 promised to be the best year yet. North Florida was far from the company's largest market—that was the North Texas Territory where I'd started my career—but I had high hopes for taking our team to the top spot.

Getting to number three had been a lot easier than any of us thought it would be. To move up, we would have to take teamwork to a whole new level and work harder and smarter than ever. No one doubted the effort would be worth it, though.

One of the biggest obstacles we would face came as a direct result of our success. Three of the guys I'd hired in my first four months in Jacksonville, including Ty, were ready to take over their own territories. In addition to what they contributed as field managers, I considered each of them a good friend I enjoyed working with. Making sure things continued to run smoothly when each one eventually left would be a real challenge.

> "You are not a leader until you have produced a leader who can produce other leaders."[5]
> —Stan Banks

Too often, managers try to hold on to their teams. Some are trying to protect their people from failure. Others just want to protect their own paychecks. I believe a major indicator of a leader's effectiveness is the number of people he or she inspires to lead their own teams or fight for their own beliefs.

Back in Texas, I'd been terrified to send Scott to corporate. Letting people go chase their own dreams doesn't always work out that well, but someone who's worked hard and earned the chance deserves to take their shot. Having these three managers—who all shared the same mission of helping people find and achieve their dreams—working as TSMs in other parts of the country would, in reality, quadruple my efforts and reach areas I'll never see. It never occurred to me that one of those guys might replace me.

* * * * * * *

One afternoon in April I got home, changed into shorts and flip-flops, grabbed something to drink, and headed to my backyard. I love East Texas, and that's where I plan to retire one day. But in Jacksonville, I could see the Atlantic Ocean from my back porch. It only took about ten seconds for me to become addicted to the tang of salt in the air and the sharp cries of sea gulls looking for a crab dinner.

An incoming call ended my downtime before it got started. Caller ID said it was Mike Keller, the company's Southwest Region vice president. I knew Mike from my time in Dallas, but I had no idea why he would be calling.

I hit the green button. "Hello?"

A smooth Cajun voice filled my ear. "Hey, Heath. Mike Keller. How's it going?"

"Great." I still didn't know what he wanted, but we were off to a good start, I thought. "How are things in Texas?"

"Everything's good. I was just wondering if you're ready to come home."

OK. He had my attention. "You mean, like for a conference or something?"

Mike chuckled. "Not exactly. I need somebody to put the North Texas Territory back together, and I think you're the guy to do it."

Whoa! This was serious. "It was in pretty good shape when I left," I told him.

"Well, it's not now, and I think bringing in a manager everybody knows and trusts is the best way to fix it. You interested?"

I had come to North Florida with the understanding that one day I would go home to Texas. That knowledge kept me from panicking during those first weeks and still comforted me when things got tough. But this was a lot earlier than I had planned. All of a sudden, I had a difficult choice to make.

A new opportunity always gets me excited, but I'd made a commitment to the North Florida team. We were serious about being the number one territory that year. On the other hand, the North Texas Territory was one of the company's largest markets, with incredible growth potential. And, as Mike pointed out, it was home.

I still had three field managers who were ready for promotion. The territory would continue to grow and succeed—in every possible way—under the leadership of any of them. By moving, I would help at least one take the next step. The new position would be a challenge. North Texas had fallen behind while I was in Jacksonville, but what could be better than helping the organization I came up in reach its potential?

I talked with Elana, then called Mike and asked when he wanted me in Dallas. Changes happen quickly in our business, so it was only a few days before I broke the news to the territory team. For the most part, they were happy for me, but change is always bad until it proves itself good. Even though I was going home, that was just as true for me as it was for them.

Of course, there's an exception to every rule. My parents thought this change was a pretty good one as soon as I told them about it. Mom would miss having a place to stay near the beach, but she said it was worth the sacrifice.

Ty would have hurt his chances for promotion by moving right then. I would go back to Texas without my best friend, but I wouldn't make the trip alone. When it was time to leave, my dad would fly to Jacksonville and help me load up. A lot had happened since Ty and I made that first trip down Interstate 10, and even though Dad hadn't been with me on that first trip or during my time in North Florida, he had been a big part of what my team and I accomplished.

I was looking forward to the journey back up I-10 and the time I would spend with Dad.

THIRTY

SUCCESS IS IN
THE JOURNEY

Heading into Jacksonville that first time, I'd been a scared kid going off on a big adventure with his best friend. Besides Ty and me, Elana was about the only person who expected success. This time, I was headed home to rebuild a territory that knew how to win, and expectations were high.

The time on the road with my dad was a welcome break from the craziness of packing up, moving, and taking on a new challenge. It was good to talk about regular stuff and take a minute to breathe before it all started again. Twelve hundred miles flew by. Dallas wasn't East Texas, but it was close and it was familiar. It didn't take long to get settled in.

Setting up one-on-one appointments with each of the territory's field managers was one of my first priorities. We talked about their concerns, expectations, and goals. Before leaving any of those meetings, I made sure I understood what that manager needed from me to help him or her, and their teams, succeed.

Based on that input, I focused on making the changes they felt were needed. I also set up the systems I used in North Florida, thinking they would work just as well for the team in Texas. I wanted to get things off to a fast start, so I planned to roll everything out at a quarterly managers' meeting scheduled for about two months out.

The fact that it had taken more than two years to develop and implement those systems in North Florida never crossed my mind.

My new regional instructor and territory recruiter bought in to my plans right away. They knew the success we'd had in Florida, and they knew what the same results in Texas would mean for them. That was important, because it was up to them to get new agents started on the right track.

> Always plan for plans to not go according to plan. Crews who consistently win sailboat races know they will get off course, and they have a plan to get back on track. The crews who think they won't ever make a mistake are likely to spend too much time figuring things out while their competition is always moving forward.

When the quarterly meeting rolled around, I was excited. I was nervous, too. Some of those field managers had been with the company nearly as long as I'd been alive. Most of them seemed receptive, and I left the meeting feeling great about what we were going to accomplish.

Except I blew it. I don't mean I blew it a little bit. I mean I really, really *blew* it. That quarter turned out to be the worst

I'd had as a manager. We didn't come close to our goals. The numbers rocked my world. Everybody had seemed excited about the new systems, but no one implemented them. Without leadership, good ideas don't translate into good results.

That two-and-a-half-year learning curve in North Florida had spun around and bitten me on the backside. Changing the direction of an organization as big as the North Texas Territory was going to take a lot longer than two months. Trying to make it happen that quickly was a boneheaded move. I hadn't given anyone time to learn the new systems, much less adjust their businesses.

This was not the big homecoming I'd looked forward to. The people who doubted me all shook their heads and patted themselves on the back. They always knew I was too young, not educated enough, or whatever. Four years earlier, I might have agreed. Just like failing the insurance exam for the third time, that kind of setback would have devastated me. I would have kept on keeping on, but I would have stewed and fumed while visions of failure and devastation danced in my head.

Instead, I got the territory staff together, told them how I'd screwed up, and apologized. We even had a good laugh about it before we went to work making things right. The systems were good ones that still work, even today. They just needed to be properly implemented.

> Success is found in the journey, not waiting at some faraway destination.

* * * * * * *

I learned a lot about leadership and success as a field manager in Texas and a TSM in North Florida, and I'm learning a lot more as a TSM back in Dallas. One of the biggest lessons is this: success is found in the journey, not waiting at some faraway destination. Also, just like failure, success isn't permanent. It lasts only in the people we help along the way. Everything else flashes bright and fades away.

As our goals and expectations change, as we change, so do the things we use to measure our progress. It's hard to stand on a piece of ground that's constantly moving. Struggle is the one thing that's constant. Every one of us will always have obstacles to overcome. We can use them as an excuse to stay where we are and leave the world as we found it, or we can learn from our difficulties and use them to make ourselves better.

That's how we become strong enough to help others along the way. That's how we change the world. That's how we make it a better place.

The only definition of success that matters is your own. It should grow and change along with you as you move forward and learn new things.

RESOURCES

HEATH'S TOP FIVE LEADERSHIP BOOKS

The 21 Irrefutable Laws of Leadership: Follow Them and People Will Follow You, John C. Maxwell (Foreword by Steven Covey)

The 5 Levels of Leadership: Proven Steps to Maximize Your Potential, John C. Maxwell

Mindset: The New Psychology of Success—How We Can Learn to Fulfill Our Potential (Parenting, Business, School, Relationships), Carol S. Dweck, Ph.D.

The Go-Giver: A Little Story About a Powerful Business Idea, Bob Burg and John David Mann

See You at the Top: 25th Anniversary Edition, Zig Ziglar (There are dozens of printings and approaching two million copies of this book in print!)

HEATH'S TOP FIVE PODCASTS

1. MFCEO — www.themfceo.com
Andy Frisella is raw, real, and genuine. Twice a week he delivers what I call Sunday morning fire-and-brimstone preaching about the truth of success and what you have to do in order to get it. Andy is a successful business owner who made it happen the hard way. He will give you real tips and truth on how to be the CEO of your own life. When you are feeling down and need a pick-me-up, this is the podcast you want to turn to.

**2. Lewis Howes School of Greatness —
www.lewishowes.com**
Lewis Howes is a true professional and one of the best at drawing the habits and patterns of success out of his guests. Each week he features someone who has earned success in a different field: athletes, health and lifestyle entrepreneurs, business people, and relationship experts, to name a few. Lewis has an amazing ability to always ask just the right questions to give his listeners incredible information and strategies to apply to their lives. The podcast is always positive, and you really get into the minds of different types of successful people.

3. Tony Robbins — www.tonyrobbins.com
Tony Robbins is just all around one of the best in the business. You will always get what Tony is saying. I love the mind-set and psychological aspects of success he discusses. His biological and technical explanations for why we do the

things we do is fascinating, especially since most of the obstacles we face exist only in our minds. Tony won't fail to inspire and motivate you while teaching you something new.

4. National Public Radio's *Hidden Brain* — www.npr.org/podcasts/510308/hidden-brain

This NPR podcast is well produced, and I love the brain science information. The program explores the mind-sets of different people, ranging from successful athletes to an ordinary person who struggled back from a concussion and became a world-renowned pianist. The show focuses on learning about your brain, how it works, and how it affects your behavior. I believe the mind is the key to achieving our dreams in life. The more you know about how it works, the more you can control how you think and the greater chance you have for creating success.

5. National Public Radio's *Planet Money* — www.npr.org/podcasts/510289/planet-money

As you would expect from NPR, this podcast is excellent in every area. It's all about money and how it makes our world go around. Past shows have included an explanation of how money is used to move oil from the ground to our cars and how to financially track a piece of cotton all the way from the cotton gin to your favorite T-shirt. What I love most is it gives me information on all kinds of businesses and how money drives them. That information, in turn, provides great insight into how to make more money in my own business.

ENDNOTES

1. The quote from Les Brown is the title of a book: Willie Jolley, author, *A Setback Is a Setup for a Comeback: Turn Your Moments of Doubt and Fear into Times of Triumph* (St. Martin's Press, October 1999).

2. Steve Jobs, Stanford University commencement address, June 14, 2005, http://news.stanford.edu/2005/06/14/jobs-061505/ (accessed August 15, 2016).

3. Zig Ziglar, *See You at the Top* [formerly entitled *Biscuits, Fleas, and Pump Handles*] (Dallas, TX: The Zig Ziglar Corporation, 1975, 1977).

4. The quote from Sanders, a former professional football and baseball player, now a broadcaster, is extensively used on the Internet, including in various memes and at sports websites.

5. The quote attributed to Stan Banks has been used many times in leadership. It is not tied to any particular use on the Internet.

NOTES

NOTES

NOTES